Wade in the Water

Wade in the Water

Following the
Sacred Stream of Baptism

Eric E. Peterson

FOREWORD BY *Leonard Sweet*

CASCADE *Books* · Eugene, Oregon

Cascade Books
An Imprint of Wipf and Stock Publishers
199 W. 8th Ave., Suite 3
Eugene, OR 97401

www.wipfandstock.com

PAPERBACK ISBN: 978-1-5326-1279-4
HARDCOVER ISBN: 978-1-5326-1281-7
EBOOK ISBN: 978-1-5326-1280-0

Cataloguing-in-Publication data:

Names: Peterson, Eric E.

Title: Wade in the water : following the sacred stream of baptism / Eric E. Peterson.

Description: Eugene, OR: Cascade Books, 2018 | Includes bibliographical references and index.

Identifiers: ISBN 978-1-5326-1279-4 (paperback) | ISBN 978-1-5326-1281-7 (hardcover) | ISBN 978-1-5326-1280-0 (ebook)

Subjects: LCSH: Initiation rites—Religious aspects—Christianity. | Title.

Classification: BV873.I54 P58 2018 (print) | BV873 (ebook)

Manufactured in the U.S.A.   APRIL 26, 2018

Unless otherwise noted, all Scripture quotations are taken from the New Revised Standard Version of The Bible.

Permission for the reproduction of the poem, *Water*, from *The Whitsun Weddings*, by Philip Larkin, is granted by Faber and Faber Ltd.

*This book is lovingly dedicated to two groups of people—a small one and a large one:
my parents, who first brought me to the sacramental waters, and the beloved community of Colbert Presbyterian Church who taught me how to swim.*

Then just six months later I baptized her.
And I felt like asking her, "What have I done? What does it mean?"
That was a question that came to me often,
not because I felt less than certain I had done something that did
mean something,
but because no matter how much I thought and read and prayed,
I felt outside the mystery of it.

—MARILYNNE ROBINSON, *GILEAD*

Table of Contents

Foreword

Battle of the Birds: Bird in the Bush vs. Bird in the Pan

Here are the mountains and the valleys to make a shepherd cry out in delight . . . where the calls of the birds sanctify the sky.

—British poet Sebastian Barker (1945–2014)

SOME THINGS ARE FOR the birds. That phrase, *for the birds* or *strictly for the birds*, means that something appeals to those who are considered lowly, unintelligent, simple-minded, unworthy, and generally dissed and dismissed by society. Christianity is for the birds.

Jesus loved birds. He told about a God who cared for every sparrow that falls (Matt 10:29). He told his disciples to look up and consider the birds of the air (Matt 6:26), or literally birds of the sky. Since in March the swifts would come back to Jerusalem and make nests in the Temple walls, and Jesus would have watched them, he may have been referring here to the swifts. In Luke, he instructs us to consider the ravens, which harks back to the Psalms (Luke 12:24). It seems theologically fitting that The Inklings met at a pub they called "The Bird" (short for Baby and Bird, pet name for "Eagle and Child").

Not surprisingly, the movement Jesus founded has rallied around a bird as its symbol. Everyone has a national bird. Bolivia and Ecuador have the Andean Condor. Iceland the Gryfalcon; Mexico the Golden Eagle; the Philippines the monkey-eating

Eagle; the UAE the Saker Falcon; Zimbabwe the Fish Eagle; Belgium the Kestrel. Of course, the United States of America has the Bald Eagle, the bird of Zeus and the bird under which the Romans marched, as did the armies of Charlemagne, Napoleon, Bismark, and Peter the Great. The eagle is the centerpiece of the Great Seal, and on June 8, 1940 a U.S. law called the Bald Eagle Protection Act recognized the bald eagle's iconic status: "Whereas, by act of Congress and by tradition and custom during the life of this nation, the Bald Eagle is no longer a mere bird of biological interest, but a symbol of the American ideals of freedom."

Christianity has an iconic bird too: a pigeon (aka dove). Not a warrior bird, but a trash bird used for sacrifice by the poor. Christianity's other iconic animals are similarly unimpressive: sparrows, fish, donkeys, and pelicans.

As a falconer myself, who was always eager for my kids to learn more about birds and their role in our faith and in our nation, I was excited when my two youngest children, both in their early teens, came home from the Orcas Island Public School the same week singing the praises of birds. They both had studied birds, and were excited about their separate experiences.

My daughter, Soren, told me how she had studied birds with a scientist from the biology department at the University of Washington. The biologist came and spent the whole day with them, and he told them everything there was to know about birds, as she put it in her adolescent exuberance.

Then it was my son Egil's turn. Egil told me that his class hosted a visit that week from a conservationist from the Wolf Hollow Wildlife Rehabilitation Center, located on an adjoining island (San Juan Island). The conservationist taught them about raptors, specifically the bald eagle population that patrols the skies around the San Juan Islands year-round. He was excited to learn more about these majestic birds that like to fish from a tree right off our deck.

As a PhD product of a great university, whom do I immediately assume got the best education in birds? My daughter, of course. After all, she had the benefit of a scientist who dedicated a whole day of his life to teaching her and her classmates about birds.

As the two of them gradually filled me in on the details of their birding experiences, I began to have a change of mind. Simply put, you know what kinds of birds my daughter studied? Dead birds. And where were those dead birds? In a laboratory. And where in a laboratory? In a pan. And what did they spend the day doing with those dead birds in pans? Taking them apart, dissecting them.

This, of course, is the best way to get to objective truth about birds. Modern science is based on the distance of objectivity and the data from observation. The Holy Roman Emperor Frederick II (d. 1250) was called the first modern man on the throne because he tried basing decisions on observation and objectivity. For example, to find an answer to the ancient question we ask when we first come out of the body, "Who are we?" Frederick II shut a man inside a barrel and waited for him to die. A hole was drilled in the barrel small enough not to let in air, but large enough to allow Frederick to observe a human soul at the precise moment it left the body.

Similarly, René Descartes (1596–1650), often called the father of modern philosophy, spent a lot of his life cutting up animals, trying to figure out how consciousness works and how brains could support consciousness. Rational arguments alone, he realized, were not decisive to prove dualism. One day a visitor commented on how few books he had in his library. "Where are your books?" he asked. Descartes ushered the guest out of the house, into his outhouse, where a calf was being dissected. "This is my library," he said.

To be modern meant to trust in objectivity and to learn to be objective. In fact, to say someone is objective is a high compliment. But does anyone want to be treated like an object? When you treat something like an object, when you get objective, you bring under your control what you are studying and you make it submit to your authority, even to the point of slice-and-dice dissection. And of course, as the Romantics often reminded amateur scientists like prince-of-the-pulpit Henry Ward Beecher, whose study was filled

with what he called his winged gems (stuffed hummingbirds)—
you can't dissect or collect winged gems without killing them first.

Let's get back to my son and his time spent with the natural-
ist from the raptor rescue center. What kind of bird do you think
they studied? That's right, they studied a live bird. But in order
to do that, they had to go to where it lived and stand under its
nest. In other words, they treated the bird like a subject. And if you
treat something like a subject, there is no *understanding* without
standing-under.

In order to get to a place where they could stand under the
subject in question (the bald eagle), they had to get on a bus and
travel to where the bird was residing. They were the ones who had
to be willing to move, to be displaced, and to be changed in order
to take part in the transaction. To treat something like a subject is
to let it dictate the terms by which you approach it. To treat something like a subject is to defer to the subject's authority and enter
into a relationship with it. They stood under the bird, not over the
bird. They spent the day standing back, not digging in and boring
down.

As much as we expect to be treated like a subject, not an object, we don't like the word subjective. We like to be objective. That
is how we most often treat the Scriptures: objective words we can
understand if we simply dissect them correctly. When it comes to
theology, we end up fixing Jesus to the cross much as a biologist
pins a bird to a dissecting table. When it comes to science, we end
up thinking we have locked everything down and buttoned everything up. At the end of the nineteenth century, scientists were
so heady that they thought they had basically discovered almost
all there was to discover. The Prussian Patent Office closed down
because it believed there were no more inventions to be made, and
President McKinley's advisors recommended he shut down the
U.S. Patent Office for the same reason.

I am grateful for higher critical scholarship on the Bible—the
bird in the pan, if you will. But it's time we learned to do bird in a
bush. We have spent so much time in the lab taking apart the bird
in the pan, we have bird flu. A bird made up of bits will never fly,

and for this culture there is no burning bush without the bird in the bush. If you want a faith-garden filled with songbirds and butterflies, you need to treat the bird like a subject, not just an object.

We have to see the life in the story and provide the soundtrack for it. Of course, in order to do this, we have to know the story. We have to know it in a way that it is living and moving and not dependent on us. It's got to be a bird in the bush, not just a bird in a pan. Because, again, when you dissect something, you necessarily kill it.

It's not our job to make the Scriptures come alive, because the Scriptures are alive. This is the living story. What we do is see the life and bring people awake so that they can come in contact with what is living.

"Bird in the bush" is a whole different way of reading the Bible than "bird in the pan." As opposed to taking things apart, we are connecting dots. When the Bible was written, the authors were not writing in chapter-verse format. We did that so we could make points out of it. But God did not send us a point to make. God sent us a person to know. Because of Jesus, we no longer live a statement, or a sentence, or a paraphrase, or a parenthesis. We live a story.

Eric Peterson's book, *Wade in the Water*, tells the whole story from the window, and mirror, and magnifying glass of baptism. He has written a bird-in-the-bush book while not ignoring the bird-in-the-pan scholarship. In what I believe is the best one-volume treatment of baptism written in the past hundred years, Peterson demonstrates that baptism is not a one-time event, but a lifestyle that makes baptism endlessly meaningful. Not to understand baptism as a daily sacrament is for Christians to leave their own story for someone else's story. When that happens, we step out of our life and disown our creator and ourselves. Here is a passage from the book that deserves to become a Christian meme and put into some iconic form as part of the great seal of Christianity:

> Baptism is the sign of the divine autograph, inscribed, not on pages, but carved in hearts. The baptized are the living signatures of the author and the editor of our faith. Moreover, the collective church community comprises

an autograph album, assigned with a sacred mission, revealing the signs of God's presence, marking the world with the indelible ink of water. Or, to rotate the prism slightly, God is an autograph collector, and each name, once dipped in the water, is added to the Lamb's book of life (Rev 21:27). God is not satisfied until the pages are full of the personal names of the baptized, inscribed for eternity in the threefold name.

There is a passage from T. E. Lawrence's *Seven Pillars of Wisdom* (1922) where Lawrence of Arabia writes, "[N]ine-tenths of tactics were certain enough to be teachable in schools; but the irrational tenth was like the kingfisher flashing across the pool and in it lay the test of generals. I have been looking long and hard for the flash of a kingfisher's wing on the church's bird-life. Eric Peterson's book, *Wade in the Water*, is one such sighting.

Acknowledgments

FROM THE BEGINNING OF this project I have had the sense that I was standing on the shoulders of giants. From the biblical writers, to the church fathers, to modern theologians and colleagues, I have been enriched by the many thoughtful men and women who came before me, and a handful who have come alongside me. I was frequently startled to find that—just when I thought I had an original idea—it turned out to be something I unintentionally ripped off of somebody else. The voices of mothers and fathers, sisters and brothers (and in all cases both the literal and the figurative ones) have influenced me more thoroughly than I will ever know. A handful of them deserve specific mention.

The incomparable Leonard Sweet introduced me to the exhilarating world of semiotics and spoke vocation-shaping words of rebuke and encouragement into my life. His influence on my thinking is evident throughout these pages. Of particular significance for me was his strong encouragement to embrace an identity as that of "an author whose voice deserves a wider hearing."

Scott R. A. Starbuck taught me the biblical languages at Princeton Theological Seminary (that I am not fluent in them is entirely my fault), and more recently helped me to think through the philosophical framework for human teleology.

Nancy Vocature, Samuel Mahaffy, and Pam Parker (the latter two of whom have subsequently completed their respective baptisms) read early drafts of the manuscript; their love of language and keen editorial eyes improved it considerably.

Additionally, are the pastor-practitioners who generously shared their experiences of how they are recovering and innovating baptismal practices in their respective congregations:

- Paul Palumbo, Lake Chelan Lutheran Church, WA

- Roger Prehn, Trinity Lutheran Church, New Smyrna Beach, FL

- Stephen Supica, Holy Trinity Greek Orthodox Church, Spokane, WA

- Linda Nepstad and Linda Elkin, Christ Our King Presbyterian Church, Bel Air, MD

Leesa Birdsall, my colleague in ministry, has been a faithful witness to the congregation we love and serve together, as well as a steady encouragement throughout this project.

The "Michael" who is named in both chapters 1 and 6 is a composite of many people living and dead who have called me their pastor over the last twenty-seven years. The proper name choice, however, is intended to honor the uncommon friendship I enjoy with Michael King LeRoy.

My debt to them all is deep. My gratitude deeper still.

I wish to express my deepest appreciation to my wife, Elizabeth, whose consistent support and encouragement over the last several years has afforded me the time and space necessary to devote to research and writing, often at the expense of other domestic responsibilities. In her customary manner, she graciously made allowances all along the way. Our life together is an inexpressible gift—one that has expanded my understanding of the sacred and has incarnated the very meaning of redemption and joy. She lives what I have here written far better than anybody I know.

1

What Am I Doing Here?

What is the chief end of man?
Man's chief end is to glorify God, and to enjoy him forever.
—FIRST QUESTION AND ANSWER OF *THE SHORTER*
CATECHISM

Who am I?
They mock me, these lonely questions of mine.
Whoever I am, Thou knowest, O God, I am thine.
—DIETRICH BONHOEFFER

MICHAEL'S LIFE HAD BEEN a success by all standards of measurement: a long and illustrious career as a tenured professor of biology at a prestigious university; a good marriage and family life, which included three healthy, well-adjusted children; respect in civic circles; a comfortable home to live in; and money in the bank to live out his retirement years. An avid fly fisherman, he spent delightful hours on the rivers in the summer and quiet evenings tying his own flies in the winter. By outward appearances he was living a pleasant version of the American Dream.

Haunting his storied past, however, was a little-known secret harbored in and harassing his heart. Although thankfully I didn't know it at the time he came to see me, this was Michael's last shot at faith; he was giving God one final chance. The pastoral conversation that followed would determine whether or not he would continue to contend with God.

As his story unfolded, it became clear that he had done everything "right": attending good schools, publishing in the right journals, serving in civic circles, going to church, even tithing. However, after a lifetime of trying, he discovered that doing these things was not inherently satisfying, and even more disconcerting, it did not make him "right" with God. The post-vocational rhythms of his twilight years had created the space for him to finally confront his existential ghosts, leading him to realize that something was still terribly wrong. Unable to distract himself any longer from the unsettled condition of his soul, the man before me alternately wept and raged, describing how it always felt to him as if his prayers "kept bouncing off the ceiling." The traumatic event from his adolescence that had twisted his identity, deforming him from the *imago Dei* to some dastardly distortion thereof, was robbing him of an abundant way of life. He was, in other words, trapped in the living of a lie, yet still looking for liberation, hoping to be delivered into a life of truth, goodness, and beauty.

New York Times columnist David Brooks gives voice to many people who have similar struggles:

> [Y]ou spend a lot of time cultivating professional skills, but you don't have a clear idea of the sources of meaning in life, so you don't know where you should devote your skills, which career path will be highest and best. Years pass and the deepest parts of yourself go unexplored and unstructured. You are busy, but you have a vague anxiety that your life has not achieved its ultimate meaning and significance. You live with an unconscious boredom, not really loving, not really attached to the moral purposes that give life its worth. You lack the internal criteria to make unshakeable commitments. You never develop inner constancy, the integrity that can withstand popular

disapproval or a serious blow. You find yourself doing things that other people approve of, whether these things are right for you or not. You foolishly judge other people by their abilities, not by their worth. You do not have a strategy to build character, and without that, not only your inner life but also your external life will eventually fall to pieces.[1]

In my role as a pastor over the last twenty-seven years, I have been listening to people share their own personal versions of this rather universal experience. Convinced, as I am, that the God of this world is primarily about the work of redeeming the broken areas of creation, I have sought to find good-news words and metaphors to speak into bad-news narratives. That search has led me back and forth again to the enduring power of the sacraments for both their ability to restore identity, and form people as citizens of the kingdom of God.

A Tale of Two Forces

The competition for our allegiance, however, is fierce. People who care about the health of the human soul—for themselves and for others—wage a daily contest between rival forces, as represented by the contradictory values between the kingdom of this world and the kingdom of God. When it comes to instilling worth in people, the culture we live in champions values primarily related to consumption and production. These materialistic values are enormously difficult to reconcile with the biblical witness. In my ministry, therefore, I have been on a constant quest to know how best to help people to not only see themselves as holy but also to live hallowed, meaningful, and abundant lives in a broken and fearful world. That lifelong search has persuaded me that baptism is the biblical sign that both identifies people as the reconciled children of God and provides the sacramental structures out of which to live sacred lives in a sacrilegious world. Embracing this identity is the key to living a good, abundant, and meaningful life.

1. Brooks, *The Road to Character*, xiii.

Before we dive in the water, however, it would behoove us first to consider the much larger contextual issue that drives this exploration, namely, the crisis of identity that is prevalent in our culture. Various versions of Michael's struggle regularly get played out in people's lives, resulting in assorted degrees of satisfaction and discouragement, leading them in a host of directions in attempts to remedy the discontent. This is the heart of pastoral ministry; engaging others in their struggles with their own version of the big existential questions:

- What is the meaning of life?
- Do people matter?
- What in the world am I doing here?

That universal human longing for a meaningful life, or what has been described as *homo significans*, is what prompts the continual search for significance. This pursuit, of course, can assume various forms and take us in many directions.

From a philosophical perspective, we might think of this in terms of human teleology: the ultimate end or purpose for which a person exists, a chief end. A handful of historical examples will suffice to demonstrate the ubiquitous nature of questions related to the meaning of life that people have sought to answer since time immemorial.

Beginning with the Ancient Near Eastern Akkadian myth of Enuma Elish (second millennium BCE), we can detect very early attempts at providing such a *raison d'etre*. According to this primeval creation story, the purpose of humanity was to serve the gods. Consider this brief section from a stone carving identified by biblical archeologists simply as Tablet VI:

> Out of his blood they fashioned mankind.
> He *imposed service* and let free the gods.
> After Ea, the wise, had created mankind,
> Had imposed upon it the *service of the gods*–
> That work was beyond comprehension.[2]

2. Pritchard, *The Ancient Near East,* 37; italics mine.

That sense of transcendence, the awareness of "otherness," has been an enduring quality of humans—a deep, innate recognition that the solitary life, divorced from community, is ultimately unsatisfying. Serving the gods, then, amounts to work that is so meaningful as to be utterly (and *delightfully*, one might infer) incomprehensible.

Aristotle (fourth century BCE) similarly explored causation by suggesting that we do not have knowledge of a thing until we have grasped its why, that is to say, its cause. Aristotle's first three causes identify a thing's purpose as *material, formal*, and *efficient*. But it is his fourth and last category that is most helpful for people to consider, namely, his *final cause*, which he describes as the end purpose toward which it points. A seed's final cause is a plant; a sailboat might be sailing. You get the idea.

What about people? What might be the ultimate purpose for humans? When somebody comes to the end of their life, by what measure will it be determined whether or not it was a good, meaningful, and purpose-filled life? Perhaps even more crucially, what criteria for life concludes with the blessed words, "Well done, good and trustworthy slave; you have been trustworthy in a few things, I will put you in charge of many things; enter into the joy of your master" (Matt 25:21). These are the types of questions that both unwittingly and consciously affect our lifestyle choices. Grappling with such questions may be among the most critical of human endeavors since the way one answers them significantly influences the quality of one's life for good and for ill.

From an Aristotelian perspective, when one observes a ship or a glass the functions of these objects are readily apparent. Even a glancing observation reveals that in the case of a ship its utilitarian purpose is for transportation on the water, and in the case of a glass it is to function as a container from which to drink. However, when we observe people, their purposes are not so obvious and clear, given the range of possibilities.

- *Does human telos extend beyond mere utilitarianism?*
- *Who defines and determines meaning?*

- *What beliefs and behaviors comprise the so-called "good life"?*

Engaging these questions so as better to understand the intrinsic purpose of people is the task of this book.

Searching for Meaning

The Stoic philosopher Epictetus (AD 55–135) claimed that the life of the mind held the key to answering such questions: "To live in the presence of great truths and eternal laws, to be led by *permanent ideals*; that is what keeps a man patient when the world ignores him and calm and unspoiled when the world praises him."[3] Versions of this perspective appear in people who are *principled* in their lifestyles, making decisions based on values, convictions, and commitments, unclouded by feelings, and with little or no regard for the consequences of their actions. It is an ethic of "doing the right thing because it is the right thing to do."

In contradistinction to both Aristotle and Epictetus, a more fatalistic approach is represented by the philosophy of nihilism, a doctrine originating with the Greek philosopher Gorgias (ca. 483–375 BCE), which argues that life is inherently without objective meaning, purpose, or intrinsic value, thereby discounting the importance of morality altogether. The contemporary expression of this perspective is captured in the nihilistic phrase, "Life is hard, and then you die." Still, most people discard such a defeatist stance, and choose to remain engaged in a quest for meaning.

Existentialist philosophy attempts to address this chronic search for human significance, but suggests that in an absurd, illogical world we must create our own existence through rational decisions and lifestyle choices. It is a struggle well illustrated by the Greek myth of Sisyphus, who was condemned for eternity to roll a rock up a hill, only to have it roll to the bottom again each time. The story demonstrates the futility of existence, while also showing that Sisyphus ultimately finds meaning and purpose in his life by continually applying himself to the task. Undoubtedly there is

---

3. As quoted by Brooks, *Road to Character*, 30; italics mine.

virtue to remaining engaged in noble struggles. But is a Sisyphean life the best, most fully satisfying answer?

The search continues into the present inasmuch as the quest for meaning persists. Joseph Badaracco, a professor of ethics at Harvard Business School, suggests that these are perennial questions reflecting our lifelong search for significance. He summarizes it eloquently:

> Human beings seem to have a built-in "explanatory drive"—we want to make sense of what is happening all around us. In traditional societies, religion and rulers, along with tradition, gave people a sense of order and meaning. In modern societies, people supposedly get more information in a day than medieval peasants did in a lifetime, but we deal with this bombardment in the age-old way—by searching for patterns, trends, and meaning.[4]

Even with the development of increasingly sophisticated algorithms for patterns and trends, meaning remains largely elusive, and the quest goes on. In his own attempt to identify the crux of this perennial search Badaracco suggests that people find meaning in "a cause or a challenge that demands and merits their best efforts, really tests their competence and their characters, and helps them lead lives they deeply value."

Thirty years ago, social critic Wendell Berry (1934–) asked the penetrating question, "What Are People for?" In a brief essay by the same title, he criticizes the erosion of a strong work ethic due to the effects of both the Industrial Revolution and social welfare programs and attempts to answer his own question with a series of other questions about human telos:

> Is their greatest dignity in unemployment? Is the obsolescence of human beings now our social goal? One would conclude so from our attitude toward work, especially the manual work necessary to the long-term preservation of the land, and from our rush toward mechanization, automation, and computerization. In a

---

4. Badaracco, *The Good Struggle*, 44.

country that puts an absolute premium on labor-saving measures, short workdays, and retirement, why should there be any surprise at permanence of unemployment and welfare dependency? Those are only different names for our national ambitions.

In the country, meanwhile, there is work to be done. This is the inescapably necessary work of restoring and caring for our farms, forests, and rural towns and communities—work that we have not been able to pay people to do for forty years and that, thanks to our forty-year "solution to the farm problem," few people any longer know how to do.[5]

Berry, it appears, views the Genesis mandate of "caring and tilling" as the virtuous purpose of humanity. Farming, he claims, is noble work that gives people a sense of meaning; while this assertion is undoubtedly true, it does raise the question of what value people have after their working years are behind them. Does a person idling about in a nursing home have less intrinsic value than the farmer who is making hay? Or does the missing chromosome of a child with Down's Syndrome make her any less precious? What about people who are unemployed, or homeless, or disabled?

Reflecting on the value of his life as he approached its end, Oliver Sacks (1933–2015), a scientist and prolific author who contributed much to popularize neurology, revealed his perspective when he wrote, "[I]t is up to me now to choose how to live out the months that remain to me. I have to live in the richest, deepest, *most productive* way I can" (italics mine).[6] Tellingly, when confronted with his immanent mortality, Sacks pointed to productivity as the best way to live his final days. Remarkably, in an opinion piece published just days before his death, Sacks, an ardent atheist, borrowed Judeo-Christian language when he wrote:

> Now, weak, short of breath, my once-firm muscles melted away by cancer, I find my thoughts, increasingly, not on the supernatural or spiritual, but on what is meant by

5. Berry, *What Are People For?*, 125.

6. Neuman, "Oliver Sacks, Renowned Neurologist and Author, Dies at 82"; italics mine.

living a good and worthwhile life—achieving a sense of peace within oneself. I find my thoughts drifting to the Sabbath, the day of rest, the seventh day of the week, and perhaps the seventh day of one's life as well, when one can feel that one's work is done, and one may, in good conscience, *rest.*[7]

That shift in emphasis from productivity to repose indicates the surrender to a man's inevitable end, when work is no longer an option, and when death needs to be befriended and embraced.

In his incomparable and insightful way, American writer and theologian, Frederick Buechner (1926–) muses on the significant role of vocation for a flourishing life. He begins by returning to the etymology of the word, which

> comes from the Latin *vocare*, to call, and means the work a man is called to by God. There are all different kinds of voices calling you to all different kinds of work, and the problem is to find out which is the voice of God rather than of Society, say, or the Super-ego, or Self-interest. By and large a good rule for finding out is this. The kind of work God usually calls you to is the kind of work (a) that you need most to do and (b) that the world most needs to have done. If you really get a kick out of your work, you've presumably met requirement (a), but if your work is writing TV deodorant commercials, the chances are you've missed requirement (b). On the other hand, if your work is being a doctor in a leper colony, you have probably met requirement (b), but if most of the time you're bored and depressed by it, the chances are you have not only bypassed (a) but probably aren't helping your patients much either.
>
> Neither the hair shirt nor the soft berth will do. The place God calls you to is the place where your deep gladness and the world's deep hunger meet.[8]

Buechner's assessment suggests that there is no one-size-fits-all answer to the question of human telos. Indeed, even identical

7. Ibid.; italics mine.
8. Buechner, *Wishful Thinking*, 95; italics mine.

tasks can carry a variety of meaning for the people doing them. Consider, as an example, the tale of a traveler who talks with three stonecutters on a worksite in an English town. The traveler asks each what he is doing. The first says, "I'm earning a living." The second says, "I'm crafting a stone that will fit perfectly into that wall and make it strong." And the third stonecutter says, "I am helping Sir Christopher Wren build a magnificent cathedral to show the glory of God."

Do you see that? Three people, all doing the same work, but each of whom assign very different meaning to what they are doing. The first cannot see any value to his work beyond a paycheck; another views his work as merely utilitarian in nature; and still another understands it as a contribution to creating enduring beauty and sacred space. In other words, the meaning of work is lodged in how it is understood and interpreted. A cynic might attribute such variations of interpretation to spin, or propaganda, or even wishful thinking. However, viewing one's own contribution as part of a greater good is often accompanied by a deep sense of satisfaction. Still, many of us ask, "Is that all that there is for us"? We wonder, "Is work the sole and ultimate source of meaning to our lives"?

Another perspective is represented by the Swiss psychologist Paul Tournier (1898–1986) who argues that a meaningful life lies in the intimacy of relationships. We are fundamentally relational beings, he argues, and so the fulfillment of our lives occurs in the context of our interpersonal relationships. However, given our tendency to sabotage interpersonal intimacy, he writes,

> [w]hen I labour to liberate a crushed life, I am not fight-
> ing against God, but with him. Like a gardener who re-
> moves from around a plant the weeds that choke it, using
> all the care that as one of God's creatures it deserves, I
> am helping to re-establish his purpose of life. It is God
> who gave it life, and he surely wants it to flourish and
> bear fruit ... Bearing fruit means being oneself, asserting
> oneself, growing in accordance with God's purpose.[9]

9. Tournier, *The Meaning of Persons*, 227.

This emphasis on the intentionality and work required to make relationships satisfying is a perennially helpful reminder. Neglecting people, as with the neglect of gardens, can result in a host of "thorny" issues. In both cases, they require attention and care.

Reflecting on his life-altering experience as a prisoner in a Nazi concentration camp in the aftermath of his bestial ordeal, Austrian physician Viktor Frankl (1905–1997), described the meaning of life as being situated in the fundamental struggle for survival. In his estimation, the people who were not sent to the gas chambers persevered under horrendous conditions and overcame despair because of a determined resolve to live. Motivated mostly by the desire to be reunited with family members, these prisoners ferociously clung to hope in the face of brutal conditions. In his own words:

> The thought of suicide was entertained by nearly everyone, if only for a brief time. It was born of the hopelessness of the situation, the constant danger of death looming over us daily and hourly, and the closeness of the deaths suffered by many of the others. From personal convictions . . . I made myself a firm promise, on my first evening in camp, that I would not "run into the wire." This was a phrase used in camp to describe the most popular method of suicide—touching the electrically charged barbed-wire fence. It was not entirely difficult for me to make this decision. There was little point in committing suicide, since, for the average inmate, life expectation, calculating objectively and counting all likely chances, was very poor.[10]

In echoing Nietzsche's claim that a person who has a *why* to live for can bear almost any *how*, Frankl affirmed that it was love that kept him alive and love that kept him going. The memory of his wife sustained him through his tribulation, reminding him of the truth that there is no higher goal to which a person can aspire, no greater telos than love. "The salvation of man," he concluded, "is through love and in love."

10. Frankl, *Man's Search for Meaning*, 16.

Looking for Love in All the Wrong Places

In complete opposition to the forced austerity of a concentration camp, hedonism seeks fulfillment through sensual pleasure. Food, sex, recreation, and various other experiences stimulate the senses and satisfy human cravings. Among the modern mottos of a hedonistic approach to life is "if it feels good, do it, because "you only live once" (YOLO). However, as long and hard as some people will test this theory by gorging themselves on pleasure, most end up discovering the truth of what American pastor H. E. Fosdick (1878–1969) described when he wrote that "our basic problem is that we are self-centered."[11] Narcissus may have fallen headlong into a pool, but he is still very much alive and operative in people today.

A final perspective on human telos is represented by the tenacity of the African American community. Under harsh living and working conditions, slaves in America's southern states found solace in solidarity with the Israelites during their bondage in Egypt. Clinging to hope in a "promised land," and a better future (usually conceived in eschatological terms), they sang songs rich in images of deliverance. Consider this exemplary portion of one of their hymns that alludes to the baptismal waters of the Jordan River:

> Deep river, my home is over Jordan,
>
> Deep river, Lord, I want to cross over into campground.
>
> Oh don't you want to go to that gospel feast,
>
> The promised land where all is peace?
>
> Oh deep river, Lord, I want to cross over into campground.[12]

This longing and hope for a better future gave slaves the ability to persist, delaying gratification until their deliverance from earth to heaven was accomplished, through either their own death or the return of Christ. In other words, they were motivated to endure a difficult present in order to inherit a glorious future. This same

11. Quoted by Brooks, *Road to Character*, 10.

12. Carpenter, *African American Heritage Hymnal*, #605.

confidence in eschatological hope for a better future, amid a troubling present, is yet operative in the modern civil rights movement to the present day.

This handful of examples provides an historical and philosophical cross-section of evidence that human beings have been engaged in a continual process of searching for the meaning to their existence. That such searching persists into the present age, along with its accompanying angst and dissatisfaction suggests that the successful pursuit of a meaningful life is both difficult and uncommon. The consequences for how questions concerning human telos are addressed become enormous, even eternal, as is one's choice of a measurement for meaning making. Suicide represents the tragic ending to a life that has lost meaning, purpose, and hope. Evidence that suicide rates are holding steady despite the plethora of products, services, and experiences promising a better life points to the existential despair to which many people unfortunately succumb. Even more importantly, it points to the urgent need for a better answer to this age-old problem. There has, perhaps, never been a time in human history accompanied by so great a crisis of identity, making the gospel message as urgent as ever.

Unfortunately, the methods employed by the church sometimes lack the substance needed to actually bring about the transformation of our lives. For example, over a period of a few months I jotted down the one-liners I came across when driving by churches in my community. Here is a sampling:

- Umbrellas needed: shower of blessings here!
- If you give the devil an inch he will become your ruler.
- CHCH. What's Missing? UR!
- Autumn Leaves; Jesus Doesn't!
- It's not about Presents but His Presence.
- Prayer is like wireless access to God, but without the roaming fees!
- IPad? IPod? Try IPray!

These are embarrassing and shallow attempts at being relevant. Even those churches that strive to offer something more substantive risk reducing the gospel message to a slogan, as in these examples:

- We preach Christ crucified and resurrected.

- Passionate Faith and Theological Depth.

The church can and must do better.

In a world full of clichés, charming sayings on church reader boards, memes on Facebook, catchy advertising jingles, and one-liners on car bumpers, what is needed is not more cleverness or even innovation, but a recovery of a sacramental worldview. Human suffering remains normative, as does the search for meaning. What is needed is a robust theology that meets people precisely *in* their suffering. A sacramental framework has the potency to provide us with both meaning and tools for perseverance as we navigate the continuum of the human condition.

With all the options tried and still available to us, where do we hang our teleological hats in order to find meaning for our lives? Is our purpose to serve gods or God; to apply ourselves to good work; to remain engaged in worthy struggles? Is it found in loving relationships; in hedonistic pursuits, or in eschatological hope? Or is the question and the quest simply an exercise in futility? The range of responses, of course, points to the lack of universal consensus.

With all the suggested and adopted ways of being, either through intention or by default, does one sign provide the most enduring framework for living with the greatest meaning and purpose? That is the question driving this exploration. As a practitioner in the art of pastoring, I have found that exercising the gift of baptism has the ability to both reorient and repurpose people for lives of meaning and abundance.

Historically, baptism has been understood in terms of Christian *initiation*—the entry point into the community, the rite by which a person is identified as belonging to the body of Christ. This initiation, however, is only the beginning point for discipleship, and the rich images of baptism are much more dynamic than static, more fluid than solid. This book therefore explores the *living waters* of baptism as a lifelong identity in which to grow up, and a purpose out of which to live. As we shall see, nobody arrives at a point of perfection in this life. Baptism, in other words, because it is complete only in death,[13] is an invitation to the ever-living waters—a lifestyle of living wet.

In a complex world, many persuasive voices and compelling forces compete to answer the question, what are people for? In the chapters that follow, I hope to demonstrate how that question is answered by contemporary North American culture, by the biblical corpus, and by the early church. In each case I will explore their insights through the lens of baptism. I will then suggest some ways to integrate baptism for lives that are more abundant. As I hope soon becomes clear, one does not need to enter a church or even get wet to be "baptized."

One caveat about this book's own telos. Because I am interested primarily in meaning, and the lived nature of baptismal identity, I will not give consideration to the various methods of administration that have been and remain controversial and divisive for the church. For example, whether baptism should be carried out by submersion, immersion, affusion, or aspersion will not be addressed. Nor will I engage the question of whether baptism is most appropriately celebrated once or multiple times in a person's life, or if standing, moving, local, or Jordan River water should be used. However, because of the crucial role early influences play in faith formation, consideration will be given (in chapter 5) to infant baptism. Pedobaptism, as it is known, has been a controversial topic throughout much of church history, and many of the church fathers argued against it, with concessions made in the case of the immanent death of children. With few exceptions (Cyprian being perhaps the most notable among them), the fathers, with

13. Calvin, echoing many of the early church fathers, wrote, "This we must believe: we are baptized into the mortification of our flesh, which begins with our baptism and which we pursue day by day and which will, moreover, be accomplished when we pass from this life to the Lord." See McNeill, *Calvin: Institutes of the Christian Religion*, 1312.

their emphasis on the primary function and necessity of the washing away of sin, preferred believer or "credobaptism." All of these sub-topics have been the source of church conflicts, debates, and schisms. With that qualification, I wish to respectfully acknowledge the widespread diversity represented among the various traditions, all of which comprise the diversity of the body of Christ. What follows represents my own selectivity vis-à-vis the emphases and angles I consider to be worthy of deeper consideration, ones that have emerged from my vocation of pastor, entrusted with the care and the cure of souls.

Consider one final image before we take the plunge. For most of my life I assumed that the purpose of mountains was for people to reach their summits. As a young boy, I remember looking out the backseat window of a Dodge Dart, where I saw Mt. Rainier for the first time, and thinking to myself, "Someday I'm going to climb that mountain." As it turned out it was a compulsion that led me to Liberty Crest, the summit, 14,410 feet above sea level four times in young adulthood. Years later I learned that the Wonderland Trail completely encircles the lower mountain, and I completed a summer sabbatical by hiking it. Over the span of ten delightful days and ninety-three miles, I explored a variety of ecosystems, enjoyed a range of plant and animal life, and endured fierce weather conditions. At the end of the trail I found that I had become much more intimately acquainted with the mountain, an experience that deepened my appreciation for its rugged beauty and seismic power.

Just so, this book takes a leisurely and somewhat meandering route around the mountain of baptism to consider and to appreciate its massive capacity to form mere mortals into the image of God.

2

Cultural Baptism:
The Church's Chief Contender

For whatever reason, the soul is made of malleable material.
It forms itself around whatever material is informing it.
Unfortunately, the people who have the greatest influence in our
lives rarely understand the power of their words to shape who we
become. They never fully understand that what informs us forms us.
—ERWIN RAPHAEL MCMANUS, *THE ARTISAN SOUL*

. . . at this very moment, and for as long as this world endures,
everybody inhabiting it is bowing down and serving something
or someone—an artifact, a person, an institution, an idea, a
spirit, or God through Christ. Everyone is being shaped thereby
and is growing up toward some measure of fullness, whether of
righteousness or of evil.
—HAROLD BEST, *UNCEASING WORSHIP*

I HAVE A FRIEND who recently forgot to set the hand brake on her
car when she parked on a steeply inclined driveway. When she returned to her vehicle she found that it had rolled down the driveway, harmlessly crossed two lanes of traffic, and come to rest in the

ditch on the other side of the road. As her husband was relaying the story to me, and without a detectable trace of criticism, he said, "Nancy never developed those driving habits early on that, after years of practice, become instinctual." Such habits are what allow drivers to have the common experience of driving safely for miles on end, deep in thought, but with no recollection of the experience after arriving at their destination, even though they were checking mirrors, monitoring speed, and remaining alert to hazards.

Discipleship, like driving, requires such formative behaviors. Indeed, if followers of the Christ do not develop holy habits through a lifetime of practice in which behavior resonates with beliefs, we may end up worshiping (if not an outright false idol) a god who has been conflated with or compromised by the gods of capitalism, consumerism, and other forms of misplaced desire. As Leonard Sweet has recently written, "character is formed so subtly that our actions seem to be thoughtless—almost second nature."[1]

Such thoughtless formation can be either a bane or a blessing, depending on whether a person is influenced by vices or virtues, or what the Bible categorizes variously as "works of the flesh," and "fruits of the Spirit" (cf. Gal 5:22–23). For lack of critical thinking skills and astute discernment, we are subject to a host of influences capable of malforming our character. Take for example the food industry in the United States: Through steady and long-term exposure to commercial advertisements, children are growing up to embrace diets high in sugars and fats, resulting in an epidemic of obesity, along with an escalation of accompanying complications, most notably diabetes and heart disease. A long-forgotten image from the 1960s displays an infant happily drinking from a 7–Up bottle fitted with a rubber nipple, along with the caption, "We have the youngest customers in the industry."[2] This, it could be said, is the food industry's version of "infant baptism." While much subtler today, marketing strategies are no less effective in converting people early on to a fast and convenient diet that is frequently embraced and sustained for a lifetime. Practice something long

1. Sweet, *From Tablet to Table*, 77.
2. Soechtig, *Fed Up*.

enough—sometimes in as little as six weeks—and it becomes a habit.

What remains hopeful in the face of bad habits, whether they are related to physical or spiritual health, is that there is rarely a point of no return. Choices and changes can be made that represent health and holiness. Good habits can be formed, and bad habits can be reformed.

No living person is ever finished. We are ever in a state of becoming. The apostle Paul describes our life in Christ as a process of "being transformed into the same image from one degree of glory to another" (2 Cor 3:18). However, who we eventually *come* to *be* is influenced by an array of factors. Our exposure to these formative influences determines, for good and for ill, the type of people into which we develop, and the quality of life we subsequently lead. Just as we know that our exposure to carcinogens frequently leads to developing cancer, we also know that a person who grows up repeatedly being told and shown that they are loved will typically become a loving person. Both nature and nurture, in their positive and negative manifestations, shape a person's identity. While I remain keenly concerned with those environmental factors, as a pastor my interest as well as my realm of influence lies more in the virtues and characteristics of Christian discipleship. In other words, I am interested in identifying the factors that form people into the likeness of Christ.

The Letter to the Hebrews contains a singularly unique word that describes the nature of just such formation. Referring to Jesus, the author writes, "He is the reflection of God's glory and the exact imprint of God's very being, and he sustains all things by his powerful word" (Heb 1:3). "Exact imprint" is how the NRSV translates the Greek word *charakter*. It could also be rendered as "mirror image." The idea is that, as we see Jesus, we are seeing God, and the implication is that as people become increasingly well-acquainted with Jesus they grow to become more like him. With origins in the ancient world, it is an image used to describe a die used in minting coins. When the die was pressed upon the precious metal it left behind an exact imprint of the king. The meaning of the word evolved from there to refer to anything that a person is exposed to; whatever presses upon us, affects who we are becoming. This, of course, is where the notion of developing one's moral character comes from. The Jewish philosopher Philo explained the word by saying that the "soul is like wax" on which various things can make either good or bad impressions. We become what presses upon us.

I am of the belief that the liturgies of worship—broadly understood—are among the agents that have the greatest power to mint citizens for the kingdom of God, with baptism as the mint mark. We will return to this topic in chapter 4. For now, I wish to explore how the prevailing liturgies in the world, along with their attendant values and influences, are operative and effective in the formation of people for a different kind of kingdom. Without such a perspective, it is much more difficult to recognize, and then to choose, the path to becoming holy. Any understanding of the sacrament of baptism, along with an appreciation for a sacramental way of living, must be accompanied by an understanding of the contradistinctive values inherent in the surrounding culture. It is impossible for us to fully realize what we stand for until we also know what we are up against. The biblical call to repentance requires both a turning *from* and a turning *toward*. As I once heard William Willimon convincingly say, "There are no unconverted people walking around. There is no neutral ground." Everything we are exposed to, everything we participate in, forms us in some *way* for some *thing*, and that often unwittingly.

North American culture is a pitiable classroom when it comes to training people for lives of Christian discipleship. However, it is an excellent and effective environment for creating people who are (or who are becoming) devotees of the values inherent in a capitalistic economy, namely, the values of production and consumption. Fed by such things as exchange rates, output, and competition, the culture we inhabit reflects these pursuits and, by association, so do the people who embrace them. Such values, while so ubiquitous as to go mostly unnoticed, are largely corrupt metaphors when applied to most aspects of the life of faith. Said another way, these are false corollaries to baptismal identity. They might even be thought of as undercover agents, with a Faustian mission to undermine the coming of the kingdom of God.

While not new to our time and place, the clash of ethics between the kingdom of this world and the kingdom of God, if not acknowledged, can create a fusion of values, significantly distorting and compromising the distinctive demands of Christian living and its call to repentance. This chapter seeks to demonstrate how environmental factors in the culture participate in the formation of people's identity and purpose. Indeed, if the world we inhabit is understood as a classroom to train us for a particular value system, the influences on our lives can be thought of as an implicit curriculum for the formation of our very souls. Relying on the insights of some of our most astute social critics, both living and dead, I hope to provide a glimpse into the ways our secular context represents a formidable force for *cultural baptism*. By intentionally using such liturgical language it is more likely that we will be able to recognize the fierce competitive energies at work, vying for our affections, our allegiance, indeed, our very souls.

At the core of this awareness is the need to first consider the nature of desire. *Worldview* is typically the way we speak of a person's orientation to life, referring to their working assumptions about a value system: what is good, what is bad, what is desirable, and what is to be avoided. How a person arrives at those cosmological assumptions and convictions is a complex process that involves a number of factors, most of which share the common ground in the nature of desire. For something so complex (as represented by such inquiries as *Is it natural, unnatural, good or evil?*; *What are its origins, and can it be tamed?*) desire may be identified by the simple, yet penetrating question Jesus once posed to a man whose heart was full of undirected desire: "What do you want?" (John 1:38; NIV).[3] Correctly answering that question is eternally consequential, and therefore deserves considerable examination,

---

3. While the NRSV translates the phrase as "What are you looking for?" the word (*dzāteō*) is just as often rendered with images belying a sense of "desire" or "want," ultimately referring to something that is being "aimed for." Cf. Matt 12:46, Luke 17:33, Acts 16:10, 1 Cor 13:5, Gal 1:10.

for what we desire and what we seek largely dictates the kind and quality of life we will pursue, both intentionally and unconsciously.

Summarizing the dilemma posed by such an inquiry, Paul Griffiths writes,

> [W]e must begin with the fact that human desire has been deranged. Our desires have moved from order to chaos; they have been opened to the damnable as well as the beautiful. Following hard on the expulsion from the Garden (a place where both human desires and the things on which they focused were arranged beautifully and cultivated in accord with God's passions), the Bible tells us, Cain envied and killed Abel.[4]

Central to understanding the nature of desire is the sobering recognition that its telos can variously lead people to the formation, the malformation, or the actual conformation (in the sense that one thing becomes like another) of their lives with respect to God. This is why it is of crucial importance to not merely *attend* but to *direct* desire.

Lacking such intentionality, the consequence for *neglecting* desire is that it is subject to being directed and manipulated by external sources. For example, if I live with a low-grade awareness that my life is missing something, and I'm looking for ways to find satisfaction, I will be inclined to cling to both the messengers and their respective messages of how to achieve fulfillment. Additionally, if I don't know what it is I really want or need, I'll be more susceptible to suggestions of what those options might (in some cases *should*) be. This is, of course, the driving force behind a culture that runs on the three-cylinder engine of *capitalism, consumerism, and success,* turbo-charged by the universal and elusive longing for happiness. Desire has an insatiable appetite, but it will feed on the fuel of any number of pursuits from such animal drives as hunger, sex, and power, to so-called "higher" aspirations of achievement, charity, and intellectual curiosity, as but a few examples.

In order to *direct* desire appropriately, we must first have an understanding of what essentially motivates us, or what we might

---

4. Griffith, "The Nature of Desire."

call the *seat of desire*. Over and against the popularity of the Cartesian view that we are primarily thinking beings and are, therefore, shaped mostly by the information that enters our brains ("I am what I think"), I am persuaded that we are formed according to our cares: "I am what I love." In other words, we are fundamentally people characterized by our affections. Included among the crucial questions for understanding personal identity and purpose, then, are:

- *How is my love being directed?*
- *Do I love rightly?*
- *Do I love the right things?*

The objects and pursuits of our desires are what philosopher James K. A. Smith (1970–) labels "liturgies." The freshest voice on this topic today, Smith argues that we worship what we love, and it is our loves that, over time, actually form us as people to the point where "we are what we love." Understanding this both personally and theologically is what led Augustine of Hippo (354–430) to describe the doctrine of the fall as "disordered love." Recognizing that love can be (and often is) misdirected allows us to make informed choices as to the object and re-aiming of our affections.

Simply having our thoughts rightly informed isn't sufficient.[5] We cannot simply *think* our desires in the direction of godliness. Instead, personal formation takes place through the liturgies of our affections. As Smith writes,

> The intimate link between bodily practices and our adaptive unconscious is a testament to the holistic character of human persons. We are not conscious minds or souls "housed" in meaty containers; we are selves who *are* our bodies; thus the training of desire requires bodily practices in which a particular *telos* is embedded.[6]

5. This is the gross deficiency in Paul Ricouer's memorable claim that "the symbol gives rise to the thought." While true insofar as it goes, it points, in turn, to the need for sacramental signs that have the power to motivate beyond mere thinking to actual behavior. See Ricouer, *The Symbolism of Evil*, 347.

6. Smith, *Desiring the Kingdom*, 62.

Necessarily then, we must determine what best engages the body in the development of values—Christian and otherwise. Conventional wisdom suggests that we are what we eat, or what we think, or what we believe; more accurately, I am convinced, we are what we *do*, assuming that we mostly do what we love. As powerful as ideas, self-talk, and even beliefs are, it is the actual *doing* of something that most influences who we are and what we are becoming.

To understand just how this works we turn to some examples of cultural influences that are chief among the counter-formative agents opposing sacramental identity and purpose. Remarkably, in describing these operative influences, social critics often co-opt language typically reserved for distinctively Christian practices as a way to awaken us to the presence and the power of cultural liturgies. For example, Jeffrey Kaplan introduces us to "'The Gospel of Consumption" in which he takes us behind the curtain of the enterprise of modern-day American capitalism to reveal "how a 1930s-businessman made you a consumer."[7]

Kaplan describes how, in this so-called "gospel," the prophets of consumerism—as represented predominantly by the National Association of Manufacturers—launched a massive public relations campaign called the "American Way." "The purpose of the campaign was to link 'free enterprise in the public consciousness with free speech, free press and free religion as integral parts of democracy.'" This commingling of values has effectively integrated the values of the two kingdoms without distinction, often assigning the biblical language of "blessing" with the accumulation of possessions. In fact, part of the campaign was to reframe language in political terms. A booklet put out by an advertising agency claimed that under "private capitalism, the *Consumer*, the *Citizen* is boss . . . and he doesn't have to wait for election day to vote or for the Court to convene before handing down his verdict. The consumer 'votes'

7. Kaplan, "The Gospel of Consumption and the Better Future We Left Behind," 40. The author references a 1929 magazine article written by Charles Kettering, director of General Motors Research, called "Keep the Consumer Dissatisfied." He wasn't, as Kaplan clarifies, suggesting that inferior products be produced. Rather "he was defining a strategic shift for American industry— from fulfilling basic human needs to creating new ones."

each time he buys one article and rejects another."[8] This appears to be the origin of popular phrases used today such as "voting with my feet," and "voting with my pocketbook."

An inherently political assumption, in the order of *inalienable rights*, accompanies the American Way of consuming even our choices. Such consumer choices might even be considered "patriotic." After one hundred years of hearing this pervasive message, most people believe it unquestioningly. Moreover, it has created important roles in our society both to maintain and to pass on the "faith."

Providing a similar point of historical perspective on how we got here, the authors of *Slow Church* write:

> After World War I, corporations that had grown rich and powerful churning out war material and other mass-produced goods grew concerned about overproduction, concerned that the American people would be satisfied with what they already had. If people stopped buying things, the factories would go quiet and the boom years would be over. Paul Mazur, a prominent banker who joined Lehman Brothers in 1927, articulated the corporate response this way: "We must shift America from a needs to a desires culture. People must be trained to desire, to want new things, even before the old have been entirely consumed. Man's desires must overshadow his needs."[9]

This bears no faint resemblance to the counter-kingdom strategy of an evangelist in service to the god of capitalism, raising up disciples of consumption through the redirection of desire.

Recognizing how people have intentionally been conditioned for an identity of consumerism, American media theorist Douglas Rushkoff (1961–) offers the following observation:

> Of course, the consumer must never be allowed to reach his goal, for then his consumption would cease. The

8. Kaplan, "The Gospel of Consumption and the Better Future We Left Behind," 43.

9. Smith, *Slow Church*, 180.

consumer must never feel completely at home in his present, or he will stop striving toward a more fully satisfied future. Since consumption makes up about half of all economic activity in America, a happy consumer would spell disaster. Fashion must change, and products must be upgraded and updated. In order for the economy to grow, this must keep happening faster.[10]

To accomplish the goal of creating consumers, persuasive influences are needed. The best evangelists and disciplers in our society are our retail stores, fortified with elaborate and well-funded marketing campaigns. The retail industry has effectively replaced the rabbinic tradition in the formation of personhood. The masterminds behind this massive machine of formation are the marketing evangelists with messages like, "Reimagine your life if you were to be in this car, in this house, in these clothes. How amazing it would be!" This is why celebrities become such important icons in secular discipleship—we associate their good looks, wealth, popularity, and success with the products they endorse. This same observation led Peter Stanford to write that "virtually every cultural influence that youngsters are exposed to—whatever the efforts of their parents to filter them—is about acquiring, possessing and hence shopping." Perhaps we are living in an age of Revivalism after all!

With the prescience of a prophet, Max Weber (1864–1920), the historical sociologist, predicted a related economic trend in the early twentieth century. However, and somewhat ironically, he was able to see how religion in general, and the Protestant Reformation in particular, played a key role in the rise of today's business world with its reliance on consumerism as its lifeblood, even going so far as to credit—or blame—the Puritans with having created the suitable "soul" for capitalism. Recognizing the dangers that would result if left unchecked, he wrote,

> The impulse to acquisition, pursuit of gain, of money, of the greatest possible amount of money, has in itself nothing to do with capitalism. This impulse exists and

10. Rushkoff, *Present Shock*, 167.

> has existed among waiters, physicians, coachmen, artists, prostitutes, dishonest officials, soldiers, nobles, crusaders, gamblers, and beggars. One may say that it has been common to all sorts and conditions of men at all times and in all countries of the earth, wherever the objective possibility of it is or has been given. It should be taught in the kindergarten of cultural history that this naïve idea of capitalism must be given up once and for all.[11]

Capitalism, one might say, capitalizes on desire, redirecting our affections, with money as its lover. Little wonder that Americans have been known to refer to currency in the somewhat blasphemous language of the "Almighty dollar."

More recently, David Byrne made a similar, personal observation regarding the way people have been formed as consumers, accompanied by this unsettling realization:

> Now everyone has at least some understanding of the fact that they are being marketed to. Sometimes we still believe that we have magically "discovered" something, but more often we are vaguely aware that someone made an effort to bring that artist or music to our attention. When I first noticed these hidden forces at work, I felt a little disillusioned. Realizing that something I really liked had been sold to me made me feel like some part of my free will had been usurped. I began to question the whole idea of free will and personal agency in my likes and dislikes—were they all manipulated according to someone else's plan?[12]

Indeed, we may be more conditioned than we would like to admit for identities as consumers through the spellbinding influences of marketers.

This peek behind the scenes of a massive, long-running propaganda campaign, directed by corporations and their marketing evangelists, reveals the forces still at work to convert people to the *American Way*, as defined by patterns of consumption and

11. Weber, *The Protestant Ethic and the Spirit of Capitalism*, 17.
12. Byrne, *How Music Works*, 215.

acquisition. This—I believe it is important to reiterate—is no slight bastardization of the *Jesus Way.*

In addition to the ways people are being immersed in and formed by consumer values and practices, baptism itself, as representing the holy alternative, has been misappropriated for secular, if not outright sacrilegious, purposes. Two examples, from two contemporary women—a politician and a performer—will suffice to demonstrate how baptism can be co-opted, though distorted and misused.

Criticizing so-called "liberal" politicians for being soft on threats to the American Way of life, Sarah Palin, speaking at a "Stand and Fight" gathering of the National Rifle Association, said, "If I were in charge they would know that waterboarding is how we baptize terrorists."[13] After thunderous applause, she went on to "thank God . . . " This conscription of biblical language for a political agenda, while nothing new, represents a gross distortion of values. The mere suggestion of associating the sacrament of baptism with torturing one's enemies is egregiously offensive to Christian orthodoxy, reminiscent of a line in Moby Dick attributed to Captain Ahab when he tempered a barb in blood: *Ego non baptizo te in nomine patris, sed in nomine diaboli!* ("I do not baptize you in the name of the Father, but in the name of the devil!"). The comment prompted the Reverend Ron Stief, executive director of the National Religious Campaign against Torture, to rightly condemn Palin's comparison of waterboarding and baptism as "sacrilegious," and called upon her for an apology.

To see just how welcomed into the proverbial henhouse the cultural fox has been made to feel, one need look no further than one of today's pop icons. Lady Gaga, as much a priestess as an entertainer, has intentionally enlisted language previously reserved only for theologians:

> "Pop culture is my religion," she has remarked on several
> occasions, and it is a religious tradition she exegetes with
> flair; her music and imagery mine the canonical texts of
> Bowie, Madonna, Elton John, and Prince, along with the

13. Blake, "Palin: 'Waterboarding is how we baptize terrorists.'"

sacred cultural repositories of sci-fi, glam, horror, high fashion and pop art.[14]

Moreover, it isn't just the culture she exegetes. Borrowing biblical language and images on her album, *Judas*, she states ever-so-blatantly, "Let the cultural baptism begin!" Additionally, a view of one of her music videos depicts her as alternately sprinkled, then immersed in water. This is, indeed, one of the high priestesses of cultural baptism, and a reminder of the ways the sacrament can be co-opted for secular purposes.

As Smith reminds us, fundamental to an honest evaluation of how cultural values "baptize" us is an awareness of what we love. And as chronic idolaters,[15] we have the capacity to love and to worship virtually anything, money being perhaps the perennial favorite. Significantly, money is a subject the Scriptures address with some frequency, warning of its grave, even mortal dangers, particularly when it becomes the primary object of our affections. The most explicit example is Paul's admonition to Timothy and to those under his care:

> But those who want to be rich fall into temptation and are trapped by many senseless and harmful *desires* that plunge people into ruin and destruction. For the *love* of money is a root of all kinds of evil, and in their eagerness to be rich some have wandered away from the faith and pierced themselves with many pains. (1 Tim 6:9–10; italics mine).

Because of its insatiable appetite, capitalism requires an ever-expanding economy to be sustainable, and consumerism is the fuel that keeps it growing. It is a force, furthermore, that has far-reaching effects.

Consequential to the ever-present landscape of consumerism is the expansion of virtually everything from houses to waistlines. Big box wholesale stores encourage people to purchase more than

14. Potter, "Lady Gaga: Monstrous Love and Cultural Baptism."

15. Calvin described the nature of humanity as "a perpetual factory of idols." See *Calvin: Institutes of the Christian Religion*, 108.

necessary, to overindulge, to acquire well beyond actual needs. Fast food restaurants, similarly, urge us to "supersize" or to "go big." The underlying marketing strategy of appealing to a desire for "more" is the exploitation of our restless hearts, and the goal is the financial bottom line. Humorously, some people have taken this pursuit to a bizarre level of application. In an artistic movement known as "more-ing" or "a new kind of more" people can be found wearing multiple pairs of suspenders and underwear; basketball "trees" arranged with half a dozen baskets; cars with a sequence of identical hood ornaments; or doors with symmetrically installed deadbolts, most of them, presumably, non-functional.

As consumer values become increasingly normative in the ethos of our society they inevitably affect our churches as well. It therefore comes as no surprise that some congregations have followed similar trends, becoming so-called "mega churches," where even the buildings look more like warehouses than worshipping centers, and their missions, while not so explicitly stated, devolve into roles as "purveyors of religious goods and services." Slick marketing campaigns and other trends borrowed from the business world, I contend, have done little to lead people either down the path of righteousness or into deeper interpersonal relationships.

Reinforcing this concern that we are affected by what we are exposed to and what we practice, recent neurological research reveals the notion that we become what we do. The repetition of physical experiences forms neural pathways, creating habits of familiarity. James Geary summarizes the science:

> Sensations, objects, and experiences repeatedly occur together with internal states, thereby becoming linked in our minds . . . The more often clusters of neurons respond together, the stronger the connections among them become. If specific neuronal groups respond repeatedly over time to the same stimulus—anything to do, say, with Halle Berry—the connections become fixed. In neuroscience, this is known as the "neurons that fire together wire together" axiom.[16]

16. Geary, *I Is An Other*, 96.

As we have seen, the liturgies in our world, habituated over time, and particularly as they shape the liturgical rhythms of our churches, form us for lives that are more suited for citizenship in the kingdom of this world than the kingdom of God. That we are so deeply embedded in the world, so "at home" in this culture, results in this formation taking place in us often unawares. An understanding and a more conscious awareness of this covert phenomenon at work and in play is essential for people who are interested in being formed more fully in the way of Christ. Consumption, production, and popularity: these are the ingredients of a cultural baptism that essentially says, "this is what you need in order to live the Good Life." Far from being merely benign or even indifferent, these influences are enormously consequential for the quality of life a person is to have. Whether we know it or not— and mostly we don't—we are being continually, intentionally, and passionately baptized. This immersion in and exposure to cultural liturgies forms us more for consumerism than for Christianity.

Moreover, our baptism into cultural values not only forms us to become more dedicated and loyal citizens of the kingdom of this world but it also creates a simultaneous resistance to Christ and the values of his kingdom. We cannot serve two masters at the same time, and we cannot hold dual citizenship in two kingdoms. A double-sided choice of resistance and surrender is required.

To summarize, individual Christians in particular, and the body of Christ as a whole, must recognize that the church exists in an environment that frequently contains values that clash with those of the kingdom of God. Because of the incongruous relationship between the culture and the church, only a growing recognition and an ongoing vigilance of these two distinct value systems will allow us to eschew the one in favor of the other.

As usual I agree with Walter Brueggemann, when he said, "My charge would be to develop a well-informed critical capacity in order to see that what we regard as 'given' in our society is in fact a construct. When recognized as a construct, alternatives become imaginable and possible."[17] I would add that it is only with such a

17. Ken Wytsma, "Sabbath as Resistance: An Interview with Walter

critical awareness that we are in a position to first choose, and then to participate in, the kind of baptism that will be formative of the kind of persons we wish to become.

What is clear is that the lifestyles into which the North American culture is baptizing us leave behind a trail of dehydrated souls. How is one to live wet?

Brueggemann," *Kenneth Wytsma* (blog), October 20, 2014, accessed October 21, 2014, http://kenwytsma.com/2014/10/20/sabbath-as-resistance-an-inter-view-with-walter-brueggemann/#sthash.VYXjONdN.dpuf.

3

Baptism in the Bible:
The Watery Thread

*When you went down into the water it was like the night and you
could see nothing, but when you came up again it was like finding
yourself in the day. That one moment was your death and your
birth, that saving water was both your grave and your mother.*
— CYRIL OF JERUSALEM

*I do not want you to be unaware, brothers and sisters,
that our ancestors were all under the cloud, and all passed through
the sea, and all were baptized into Moses in the cloud and in the
sea . . .*
— FIRST CORINTHIANS 10:2

"STUDY THE SCIENCE OF art," Leonardo Da Vinci once advised.
"Study the art of science. Develop your senses. Especially, learn
how to see. Realize that everything connects to everything else."[1]
The Renaissance Man didn't know it at the time, but he was referring to what would later be known as semiotics: the study and

1. Leonardo Da Vinci, *Notebooks*, n.p.

33

science of signs, the recognition that "everything connects to everything else." To grasp the concept, begin by imagining yourself
standing in the middle of a stream while the water flows by your
legs. The stream represents all that is—past, present, and future.
The particular place and point in time in which you stand is the
present moment; it is fleeting, always changing, emerging from the
upstream future, and flowing into the downstream past. In an in-
stant, the future becomes the present, and just as quickly gives way
to the past. Of course, the "present" depends entirely on the fixed
point at which you happen to be standing at the time.

If you are historically informed about what has been floating
by you, and if you are alert to the signs in the present moment, you
can begin to anticipate what is coming from upstream, even before
you can see it. There is one, long, cosmic stream of life and death,
and it is all interrelated. That's semiotics: everything connects to
everything else.

For example, in this moment, when you read the word *bird*
it doesn't get stuck on the page because you see not the word itself
but the image of some avian species it suggests for you. The word
takes flight as you recall the memory, perhaps, of a red-tailed hawk
soaring overhead. Connecting the word on the page to the bird in
the sky is what semiotics does. Words, as signs, represent things.
Semiotics is sign language.

Similarly, there are some things that represent other things.
Sacraments are characterized by ordinary things in this world
that point to the extraordinary realities of the kingdom of God.
Something as simple and common as the combination of bread
and wine, for example, has come to be powerfully associated with
the body and blood of Christ. Additionally, the act of eating and
drinking the eucharistic meal is a way for the church of Jesus Christ
to commune together with the Spirit of the risen Lord. Through
it, we participate in the life, death, resurrection, reign, and return
of Christ. Sacraments have a mysterious way of converging and
collapsing in time the saving acts of God, past, present, and future. They recall God's faithfulness and anticipate God's promises

fulfilled, and they do so in the particular and mysterious moments in which the sacraments are celebrated.

Baptism is the sign by which the dots of a person's life are connected in the lifelong journey of discipleship. It is the mark by which we are identified as the chosen children of God. Baptism, I suggest, is the chief semiotic of the Christian faith, from beginning to end. Reading and understanding this sacramental sign is the key to living a holy life.

I love how Frank Griswald has managed to capture the way baptism represents the simultaneous dynamic of beginning in Christ and growing in Christ: "Baptism," he says, "is both a discrete event in a person's life and a life-long process of 'growing up in every way into him who is the head, into Christ' (Eph 4:15) and acknowledging with St. John that 'what we will be has not yet been revealed' (1 John 3:2)."[2] The beauty and the intrigue of baptism lies in its fathomless depth of meaning, as well as its wide-ranging implications for a life of discipleship. The word *fathom* by the way, while it is typically used as a unit to measure the depth of water, originates in the sense of "something that embraces," or "with outstretched arms." Thus, while a literal fathom represents a water depth of six feet, it's a word that has significant semiotic implications for a person who embraces a lifestyle of living wet in the sacred waters of baptism. One could even say that we are seeking to "fathom" or "plumb the depth" of the baptismal mystery, and to live out of those deep, sacred waters in the lifelong "process of Christ," the continual developmental movements in the exercise of faith. We will return to this concept in chapter 4. For now, we turn to the origins of baptismal images sprinkled throughout the Old Testament so that we can connect some important, biblical dots.

Showing Signs of Promise

Nearly every promise contained in the Holy Bible is accompanied by a sign. God makes a promise, and seals it with some kind of a

2. Griswald, *Drenched In Grace*, 218.

sign as a reminder of that promise. Noah was the first recipient among many who received such a two-part gift when God made the promise to never again destroy the earth with a flood. That initial covenant of blessing was (and is) paired with the sign of the rainbow. The joining together of promises and signs (words and sacraments) are God's way of establishing and maintaining covenant with his people. Call them *promisigns*.

The biblical promisigns deal primarily with the notion of beginnings and becomings. Nearly everything that God initiates has intentions in perpetuity. Thus, the signs that have historically accompanied God's covenantal promises are with us to this day, things like rainbows, circumcision, tablets, bread and wine, and, most notably for the purposes of this chapter, water. In each instance, but culminating in the promisign of baptism, the holy invitation is to begin a new life with Christ, and to grow to be like Christ. A number of baptismal allusions located in the Old Testament, can be semiotically connected to New Testament texts. We begin there, by following the water.

Creation: (Re)Signing Order out of Chaos (Genesis 1-2)

The first sentence of the Bible ends on a wet word: "In the beginning when God created the heavens and the earth, the earth was a formless void and darkness covered the face of the deep (*tehōm*), while a wind from God swept over the face of the waters (*mayim*)." Significantly, according to the first creation account, five of the six days of creation include references to water (day four, with its focus on the lights, is the notable exception). But it doesn't end there. By the end of Genesis 2 there are more than twenty-two references to water. Water is the source, the beginning, the very genesis of all life. It is the sacred stuff, in other words, of beginning and becoming.

The nature of these waters is described by the writer as *tōhû wābōhû*. Typically translated as "a formless void," the Hebrew phrase points to something that is hard to fathom, like nothingness squared; it is dark, moist, fertile—much like a womb—an environment readied for the embryonic development of life. Water is the primary source of our existence.

These inchoate and chaotic waters from which creation began are evocative of deep mystery and refer to a fertile environment for birthing. It is actually not a big etymological stretch to describe them as seminal fluids, the hydroponic seedbed of life. Gregory of Nyssa was the first to make this connection, showing the cause and effect relationship between the life-giving sperm and the person who resulted. "Even as the power of God takes the moist sperm and makes a human being, so the power of God uses the water of baptism to make a corruptible human being into an incorruptible person."[3] Baptism hearkens back to these primal, procreative waters as the essential sign of the new creation in which God reclaims lives and restores relationships, time and again bringing order out of chaos.

Garden: Sign of Our Origins

The second creation story (though believed to be an earlier version) is located in the center of a garden watered by a stream. The text says that God formed man from the dust of the ground, but anyone familiar with the art of sculpture knows that dust needs to be mixed with some water in order to actually give it form, much like clay needs to be moistened before it can be shaped. It appears, then, that the ingredients used in the making of humanity were the dust of the ground, the breath of God, and water.

There is a clear semiotic relationship that connects the combined creation stories to a unique gospel incident located in John 9. Just as Genesis 2 depicts God kneeling down in the dirt (*adamah*), forming Adam from a mud pie, so too Jesus imitates this creative act by spitting on the dirt, making a mud pie, smearing it on the blind-from-birth man's eyes, and restoring his sight, recreating him in the *imago Dei*. With this one addition: Jesus sent

3. Ferguson, *Baptism in the Early Church*, 609; Ferguson cites Gregory of Nyssa, *Catechetical Oration* 33, 34, 40, *GNO* 83, 15-16; 85, 9-10; 103, 9-10.

the man to the pool of Siloam to get wet. In other words, the Sent One (*apostolos*) sent a blind man to a pool named "Sent" where he was healed, and then sent him back into his community to tell his story—one that has become something of a classic testimony: "The man called Jesus made mud, spread it on my eyes, and said to me, 'Go to Siloam and wash.' Then I went and washed and received my sight'" (John 9:11). For this unnamed blind man, his first seeing day marked the holy occasion of not only his healing-via-hydrotherapy but his genesis of becoming an apostle—sent to speak good news. This is both the signature work of Jesus, and the characteristic sign of our re-creation.

Similarly, one of the easy-to-overlook apostles is introduced to us in John's Gospel when Jesus interacts with a woman of Samaria in another watery text. The story, you may recall, is introduced by the Pharisees' observation that "Jesus is making and baptizing more disciples than John" (John 4:1). The word John uses here for water (*hudōr*) appears no fewer than nine times in this story, alluding to its baptismal significance. Even without the mandate of being "sent" to proclaim good news she nonetheless "left her water jar and went back to the city, and said to the people, 'Come and see a man who told me everything I have ever done! He cannot be the Messiah, can he?'" As a result of this unlikely apostle, one who received a new beginning around Jacob's Well, and was sent to bear witness to her encounter with the Christ, "many Samaritans from that city believed in him" (v. 39). Significantly, this story also concludes on a wet note as John shows Jesus then moving on to Cana, reminding his readers that this is "where he had changed the water into wine" (v. 46).

Returning briefly to the Genesis 1 account, we find there a description of the first day of creation involving the introduction of light to the world, which is later reflected in both the life and the words of Jesus when he said, "as long as I am in the world I Am the Light of the world" (John 9:5). In the great irony of the story, of course, a once blind man ended up *seeing* Christ more clearly than all the Pharisees combined, since their view of the truth remained limited to the Law of Moses (v. 28).

Noah: Sign in the Sky (Genesis 6-8)

The story of the Flood is a pivotal one for understanding both the lethal and the life-giving attributes of baptism. God's decision to use a deluge to "blot out from the earth" both the human beings and the animals he had created was prompted by the wickedness that was running rampant at the time. This is the second indication that God takes sin seriously and deals with it definitively, the first involving the banishment of Adam and Eve from the Garden of Eden.

Fortunately, death is never the final word in God's story. Recognizing the righteousness of Noah, God preserved a remnant to participate in a divine do-over. Buoyed above the destructive forces of the floodwaters, Noah and his shipmates of family members and animals were saved from death, preserved for life in the first Ark of the Covenant. Like baptism, the flood story depicts an inner and an outer dynamic in which the container of the ark and the container of our bodies are wet on the outside, washed of sin, while simultaneously being dry on the inside, a safe sanctuary where salvation is effected. Then, with the receding waters came God's promise of "never again," followed by the arc of the rainbow that became the sign in the sky of this covenant promise: a promisign that yet today recalls the great story of the Deluge, and reassigns it as the story of God's great Flood of love, inviting the baptized to live in the flood plain of grace. Baptism, moreover, is the modern-day invitation to reenter the lost ark by a once lost people, who are now found in the saving grace of God, the one who is yet preserving a remnant[4] people, not for destruction, but for salvation.

The Apostle Paul, influenced by the prophet Isaiah, picked up on this theme in his letter to the church in Rome, writing, "Though the number of the children of Israel were like the sand of the sea, only a remnant of them will be saved" (Rom 9:27). And again, "So

---

4. The first use of this word occurs in Gen 45:7 when Joseph reassures his brothers, saying, "God sent me before you to preserve for you a remnant on earth, and to keep alive for you many survivors."

too at the present time there is a remnant, chosen by grace" (Rom 11:5). By referencing the small fraction of the world's population that was saved in the ark, Paul is indicating that the water of baptism is yet preserving a remnant people for life. Likewise, the Apostle Peter picked up on this vivid image descriptive of remnant theology when he wrote of "God waiting patiently in the days of Noah, during the building of the ark in which a few, that is, eight persons, were saved through the water. And baptism, which this prefigured, now saves you" (1 Pet 3:20–21).

Moses, more often associated with the Ten Commandments, reflects this notion of preservation-via-lifeboat when his mother waterproofed a papyrus basket and buoyed him out of harm's way in the Nile River. As the story goes, he was later adopted by Pharaoh's daughter who named him *Mosheh* because "[she] drew him out [*mashah*] of the water" (Exod 2:10). The boy who, like Noah, was saved by floating on water, grew to save a whole nation of people by leading them through the parted waters of the Red Sea, from a condition of Pharaoh-imposed slavery into a land of promise, and ushered them into a life of freedom (Exod 14). Again, it is worth noting the lethal *wet* and life-giving *dry* images associated with this story, where the waters are first parted for the Israelites, granting them safe passage for life, and ushering them into a land of promise, followed by the waters crashing in upon the Egyptian army destroying them as the enemies of God's chosen people.

Additionally, the story of deliverance from Egyptian bondage to the promise of freedom was remembered not so much as one of mere rescue, but of joy. Indeed, the dominant tone of the Passover celebration to this day is accompanied by a spirit of delight. My father, Eugene Peterson, commenting on the book of Ezra, observes that

> Passover wasn't a somber ceremony but a celebration. Rather than being sprinkled in a stoic ritual with smatterings of God's grace, the Jews were plunged into a sea of joy, coming up from their immersion in God's grace, splashing gleefully together in the water.[5]

5. Peterson, *Conversations*, 665.

One could hardly find a more appealing image for baptism!

Abraham: Sign in the Flesh (Genesis 15-17)

While Captain Noah was the recipient of a promise of *preservation*, Father Abraham received the gift of *multiplication*, a covenant promise that was accompanied by the sign of cutting. While covenant-making rituals commonly involved the cutting of animals (or in the case of Moses the cutting of stones), the Abrahamic promise was sealed with the sign of cutting some flesh—his flesh.

The promise it pointed to was that he would become "the ancestor of a multitude of nations." For reasons that are never explained, God identified Abraham—in his old age no less—to be the patriarch of a people so numerous as to exceed the grains of sand. Unlike Noah, who seems to have been chosen precisely because he was a righteous man and "found favor with God" amid the great wickedness that had come to pervade the earth, Abraham appears not to have stood out in any significant way. In fact, there is no mention of Abraham's righteousness until *after* the promise was given to him one starry night when God invited him to, "Look toward the heaven and count the stars, if you are able to count them. Then he said to him, 'So shall your descendants be.' And he believed the Lord; and the Lord reckoned it to him as righteousness." Abraham, it would seem, grew into righteousness as he lived into this covenant, much like latter day heirs to the promise come to the waters of baptism unworthily, and live into their identity as children of God. The Apostle Paul later pointed back to this example as a way to demonstrate the ways God justifies his people, writing,

> We say, "Faith was reckoned to Abraham as righteousness." How then was it reckoned to him? Was it before or after he had been circumcised? It was not after, but before he was circumcised. He received the sign of circumcision as a seal of the righteousness that he had by faith while he was still uncircumcised. (Rom 4:9–11)

Circumcision, as Paul reminds us, was the sign of the multiplication promise given to Abraham. Because of the human anatomy involved it is a topic that has often been too quickly, bashfully turned away from, avoided out of embarrassment. Yet that is almost the point: it is so intimate, and so sensitive as to remind us that our life in Christ—far from being some sort of super-spiritual, Gnostic-like belief system—is deeply personal. It cuts to the quick. It meets us in the flesh. It touches a nerve. Furthermore, unlike the occasional sign of the rainbow, Abraham would have been reminded of his promise every time he *made water*, presumably several times a day, giving him frequent occasions to give thanks to God.

The way this promise began to be fulfilled was no slight thing. Significantly, only the God who made the promise could keep the promise. God chose—as the unlikely (and medically impossible) place for the birthing of this promise to take place—a geriatric womb that had failed for nearly a century. So implausible was the sound of this divine birth announcement that it caused Sarah to have a good laugh over the mere thought. But when the child was born, tickled that they were finally parents, the old couple kept their laughter alive by naming their son Isaac.[6]

If it weren't for St. Paul's theological redaction of the Abraham story we might not see this as yet another prefiguring of the baptismal covenant. While there are allusions to this in his letter to the Romans the explicit language shows up in his letter to the Colossians:

> In him also you were circumcised with a spiritual circumcision,[7] by putting off the body of the flesh in the circumcision of Christ; when you were buried with him in baptism, you were also raised with him through faith in the power of God, who raised him from the dead. (Col 2:11–12)

6. This is a play on the Hebrew words *yitschaq* (Isaac) and *tsachaq* (laughter).

7. The Greek word, *axeiropoiātos*, refers to a circumcision "made without hands."

The Abrahamic covenant, it can be said, prefigures the New Covenant as it cut out a remnant people from the world, enabling them to make the *final cut* for salvation.[8]

Moses: Sign in the Stones (Exodus 19)

Apart from his association with water, first as an infant in the Nile, and later as an adult in the Red Sea, Moses initially seems an unlikely precursor to baptism. But notably when God appeared to Moses to give him the Ten Commandments, he came shrouded in the vaporous waters of a cloud, saying to him, "Go to the people and consecrate them today and tomorrow. Have them wash their clothes and prepare for the third day, because on the third day the Lord will come down upon Mount Sinai in the sight of all the people." It is Origen, who, with his sacramental nose, helps us to see that the command to wash their clothes means that "your garments were washed once when you came to the grace of baptism; you were purified in body; you were cleansed from all filth of flesh and spirit." But Paul noticed this first, writing, "[O]ur ancestors were all under the cloud, and all passed through the sea, and all were baptized into Moses in the cloud and in the sea" (1 Cor 10:2).

Even more significant is the cutting image as it spans the two testaments, providing a semiotic way of connecting covenantal language, old and new. Most explicitly is the convergence of images demonstrated in Paul's letter to the church in Rome when he referenced Abraham and his first-covenant descendants, along with the new-covenant remnant, to show how Gentiles in Christ have been grafted (cut into) Israel—the chosen people of God (Rom 11). If one is willing to mix the physiological, the lithological, the horticultural, and the theological images, we can see that each of these promisigns is part of the whole, with the Abrahamic (flesh-cutting), the Mosaic (stone-cutting), the Pauline (branch-cutting), and the messianic (heart-cutting) covenants transplanting us into the body of Christ.

8. Cf. Rev 20:11–15.

Jonah: Sign of the Fish

The story of the minor prophet Jonah, while memorable because of its vivid, dramatic images, has been largely overlooked as a foreshadowing of baptism. But this hasn't always been the case. A favorite image found in older European baptisteries depicts Jonah rising up and out of the belly of a great fish against a watery background. For example, the bronze panel for a baptistry in Cologne, Germany makes explicit this connection. "The waters resemble the waters of baptism, the whale resembles a font, and Jonah stands as one raised to new life."

Jonah's contribution to the corpus of baptismal theology lies in the inside-out theme of destruction and deliverance. Similar to Noah and the ark, the days Jonah spent within the great fish preserved his life. Not only does Jonah's story look back to Noah's but it also anticipates Jesus, who spent three days deep within the earth. It is these relatively brief, three-day gestational periods that ushered first Jonah and then Jesus from death to life, metaphorically in the former instance, and quite literally in the latter. In Jonah's case, the reluctant prophet was swallowed alive by the great *ixthus*[9] who spit him out three days later. The man that emerged was a different man than the one who was swallowed whole. Three days in the belly of a great fish gave Jonah time to think about his life with respect to his relationship with God and his holy calling to be a mouthpiece for God. That was just enough time to change everything: his heart, his mind, his direction.

Similarly, the three days Jesus spent in hell (a baptism of fire) was just enough time to rearrange humanity's relationship with sin, and to overcome the power of death. In both cases the gestational environment for new life was a dark, mysterious place. We do not know exactly what happened in those respective "bellies," but we know that something significant transpired as demonstrated by the changes in the men who emerged, namely, Jonah came out a repentant man, as evidenced by the new direction he went.

9. The Greek word for "fish" is also a popular five-letter acronym that identifies Messiah: *Jesus Christ, God's Son, Savior.*

And Jesus came out of his tomb, ascended into heaven, and thus rearranged the spiritual forces of the universe through a cosmic turnabout, bringing to an end the power of death.

During his earthly tenure, there were numerous requests—even demands—for a sign that would validate Jesus' messianic identity. Matthew cites two typical examples: "Then some of the scribes and Pharisees said to him, 'Teacher, we wish to see a sign from you'" (Matt 12:38). On another occasion, something very similar took place when "the Pharisees and Sadducees came, and to test Jesus they asked him to show them a sign from heaven" (Matt 16:1).

According to the Synoptic Gospels, Jesus consistently resisted such tests of his identity, insisting that all the evidence they needed was already at hand. Pointing back to a little wet prophet, he said,

> An evil and adulterous generation asks for a sign, but no sign will be given to it except the sign of the prophet Jonah. For just as Jonah was three days and three nights in the belly of the sea monster, so for three days and three nights the Son of Man will be in the heart of the earth. The people of Nineveh will rise up at the judgment with this generation and condemn it, because they repented at the proclamation of Jonah, and see, something greater than Jonah is here! (Matt 12:39–41)

By invoking the memory of Jonah Jesus was giving his hearers a short-hand sign of what happens when people, upon hearing the Word of God, turn from their sin and turn to God. Just as the Ninevites will "rise up at the judgment with this generation and condemn it, because they repented at the proclamation of Jonah" (Matt 12:41) so too will those who repent of their evil ways go from being the condemned to participating in the condemnation of evil. Baptism is the sign of this flip-flopping relationship between sin and condemnation, as it incubates people for a new life in Christ, transforming them—Jonah-like—from lives and lifestyles of running away from God, to lives of running after God.

It should be noted that the Fourth Gospel describes signs quite differently, even favorably,[10] portraying them as evidence of who Jesus is. The Evangelist has no fewer than a dozen references to the miracles that Jesus performed as signs (Gk: *sēmeion*), pointing to him as the bona fide Christ, specifically including the miracle at Cana (John 2:11), the healing of the boy in Capernaum (John 4:54), the feeding of the five thousand (John 6:14), and the raising of Lazarus (John 12:18).[11] These are but a sampling of all that he did, for John tells us that "Jesus did many other signs in the presence of his disciples, which are not written in this book. But these are written so that you may come to believe that Jesus is the Messiah, the Son of God, and that through believing you may have life in his name" (John 20:30–31).

Creation, rainbows, circumcision, tablets, and a fish: these are primary among the signs pointing to the promise that we are living in an age of promise, or what is known to astrologists as the Age of Aquarius. Though located outside the realm of a Christian cosmology, the sign of Aquarius is associated with the constellation known as the Water Bearer in the cosmos, believed by some to signal a period of peace and harmony. According to astrology, we are presently living in the Age of Aquarius; we are living under the sign of water. That water is a universal theme that gets expressed even in mythology points to the sacred thirst that pervades the human condition. Whether they are signs in the skies or signs in the ground, signs in stone, or signs in the flesh, all of these signs ultimately point to Emmanuel—the incarnational sign that God is with us.

---

10. Similarly, the three initial signs that God gave to Moses (turning his staff into a snake and vice versa, making his hand alternately leprous and healthy, and transforming Nile River water into blood) were given to help the Israelites believe that God had commissioned Moses to lead them out of Egypt (Exod 4:1–9).

11. Traditionally, the church has identified seven specific "signs" in John's Gospel. In addition to those mentioned above are the stories of Jesus walking on water (6:16–35), the healing of the blind man (9:1–41), and the healing of the paraplegic by the pool of Bethesda (5:1–18).

In a world where it is easy to lose one's way, we are given these reorienting signs of promise which define and direct us toward life at its best. These promisigns point to the enduring faithfulness of God—and beyond, to the sign of the New Covenant—enacted in baptism and embodied in Christ, the focus to which we now turn by following the sacred waters as they flow into the New Testament.

Storied Waters

We usually think of the containers for stories being words, whether conveyed through voices or books, spoken or written words. However, the storied waters of baptism are a different kind of container, with the ability to rewrite and retell stories-gone-bad with a redemptive ending. Water carries God's story, my story, the community's story—past, present, and future—through the generations. It is the vehicle of good news, the agent of salvation.

Asked what they think of when invited to make an association with baptism and the Bible, most people will point to one or the other bookends of the gospel: the baptism of the Lord or the Great Commission. Mark is the gospel writer who makes the connection most explicitly, describing Jesus' own baptism in chapter 1 and his commissioning of the eleven in chapter 16: "Go into all the world and proclaim the good news to the whole creation. The one who believes and is baptized will be saved" (vv. 15–16).[12] Significantly, both of these incidents are recorded in the context of stories, suggesting to us that the baptismal story—the watery thread that meanders throughout the salvation narrative—demonstrates

12. This lesser-known version of the Great Commission located in the longer ending of Mark's Gospel is worth noting because it is accompanied by indicators to supposedly confirm the veracity of people who are saved. Jesus said, "[A]nd these signs will accompany those who believe: by using my name they will cast out demons; they will speak in new tongues; they will pick up snakes in their hands, and if they drink any deadly thing, it will not hurt them; they will lay their hands on the sick, and they will recover" (16:17–18). These signs, in other words, accompany those who are bona fide Christians. That these signs are not typical of the church in the West is something I wish to here acknowledge, but not now explore.

how this sacred narrative redeems and redirects the lives of people whose stories have gone terribly wrong. In other words, not only does it represent the overarching span of the biblical story from beginning to end, but it marks and defines, even restores (re-storys!) people within the New Covenant from beginning to end.

Notably, the gospel of Jesus Christ does not start with Jesus, but with John the Baptist, who first issued the call for a baptism of repentance.[13] It was by this sign that the arriving kingdom of God began to demonstrate how it is that God can "raise up children to Abraham" (Matt 3:9 // Luke 3:8), thereby grafting new people into a renewed covenant. The sacred waters of baptism—through their universal, expansive, global effects (including Jews and Gentiles)—floods the world with salvation, reconstituting the earth's inhabitants as the *chosen* people of God.[14]

The beginning of the good news begins with water. Mark did not start his story, the way many of us begin our stories, and the way Matthew and Luke began telling their version of this same good news story, with birth. He begins it, rather, with baptism. The beginning of good news, he insisted, begins with water—more precisely, the local Jordan River waters in which Jesus was baptized.

According to Mark's account, we don't hear the Word-made-flesh utter a blessed word until he was baptized. Not until after his baptism did Jesus formally begin his ministry of calling and making disciples. For Jesus and for all who follow him baptism celebrates both the "at-handedness" of the kingdom of God, as well as the full participation of the believers in that new way of life.

Following are five perspectives revealing how the sign of baptism, as revealed in the New Testament, is operative in the unique

---

13. St. Mark is the gospel writer who emphasizes this most notably, using baptismal language six times in the first nine verses of his account (in contradistinction to Matthew and Luke who both wait until chapter 3 to introduce the concept).

14. The underlying meaning of being chosen (Gk: *eklektos*) conveys a sense of divine favor. I contend that the "baptismal cloud" out of which the voice spoke that particular word to Jesus at his transfiguration (Luke 9:35) resounds throughout the New Testament to indicate how baptism identifies a *choice people*, chosen by God. Cf. Rom 11:5; Col 3:12; 1 Thess 1:4; and 1 Pet 2:9.

conditions of peoples' lives, each episode contributing something unique to a sacramental worldview.

John the Baptist: Sign in the Water

Echoing and recapitulating the opening phrase of Scripture, "In the beginning" (Gen 1:1), the good news of Jesus Christ, according to John's Gospel, signals its recreative purposes by calling people to return to their origins, as if to say, "it's time to begin again." Significantly, both the story of creation and the story of salvation begin with water.[15]

It is important to notice that the water in Mark chapter 1 is the same as the water in Genesis chapter 1 in order to make the necessary connection between creation and re-creation. The world contains a finite amount of water and it cycles through its life in the forms of solid, liquid, and vapor, but it is all the same water, none of it more special or holy than others. The water used in today's baptismal fonts is no newer than the water over which the Spirit of God hovered when the world was still an empty womb. The water ebbing and flowing in oceans today is the same water that buoyed Noah's ark. The water in a glass of tap water could very well contain some of the same molecules that Jesus turned into wine at a wedding in Cana almost two thousand years ago. Life begins with water. Stories of life and stories of new life begin with water.[16] Not surprisingly, then, the beginning of most everything that God initiates involves water. Our life began in water, and our new life in Christ begins in water. We are created in water, we are recreated in water, and we are regularly renewed in water.

John the Baptist was given the assignment, as the forerunner to Jesus, to prepare people to hear, to receive, and to respond to

15. The Heidelberg Catechism helpfully dispenses with any magical or even salvific associations with baptismal water, describing it as "only a divine *sign* . . . " (4.078).

16. This is why astronomers get so excited when they find signs of water on distant planets—because if there is water to be found, chances are good that there is also life.

the invitation to begin again in God's new creation by stepping into the kingdom of God. While his voice issued its prophetic call to repentance in the dry conditions of the Palestinian wilderness, the invitation was to get wet in the river that runs through it. His message, thundering from that arid environment, called people to leave behind their parched souls, by turning to the living waters.[17] John's is a timeless message of repentance in a dry land, pointing to the oasis of salvation.

As with every effective metaphor and sacramental symbol, John used something common and ordinary, and yet essential: water. While his voice bellowed a message of repentance, his hands dunked people in the Jordan River as a sign of a dramatic, definitive turnabout, as they left behind their old life—through figurative *drowning*—and embraced a new way of life in Christ with their first new breath as they emerged from the waters, refreshed, renewed, renamed in the trifold Name.[18] John the Baptist, who may well have been a product of the Essene community, with ritual washings as a centerpiece of his life, was the quintessential Aquaman.

The baptism John administered was accompanied by a clarion call to repentance. Both Matt 3:7 and Luke 3:7 report John's prophetic admonition almost identically: "You brood of vipers! Who warned you to flee from the wrath to come? Bear fruit(s) worthy of repentance." The Gospel according to Mark conveys the same message, though less directly: "John the baptizer appeared in the wilderness, proclaiming a baptism of repentance for the forgiveness of sins" (Mark 1:4). John's words and his baptism of repentance not only prepared people to receive Messiah but also prepared the church for a ministry of word and sacrament. These are the essential means of grace given in service to the gospel: in spoken words and through common matter the church is continually calling and inviting people to repentance, turning from their sins, turning to their maker. Baptism summons people to embrace

17. Cf. Jesus' self-referential language that appears in John 4:10.

18. To be sure such Christological and Trinitarian understanding can only be assigned to John's baptism subsequent to the Ascension.

a lifestyle of repentant discipleship.[19] A repenter, therefore is one who is continually engaged in the lifelong process and progress of daily transformation—both in identity and in practice—variously conceived as turning from sin to Christ, from death to life, or as one who is incarnating a palindromic lifestyle from *Evil* to *Live*. This is the essence of practicing one's baptism.[20]

Jesus: Sign of God-with-Us

Jesus was baptized. As the one person in the world, due to his sinless nature, who did not need to be, Jesus insisted on being baptized, thereby galvanizing his resolve to fully condescend as Emmanuel: an exquisite display of solidarity by God-with-us, and God-for-us, demonstrating, moreover, that it is a gift for all humanity, and not to be neglected.

On the one hand, the baptism of the Lord was an exercise in utter humility, as captured powerfully in the parallel construction of Theodotus, a fifth-century bishop of Ancyra: "The Master comes to the servant, the King to the soldier, the One who needs nothing to the one in need, the Giver to the borrower, the Reality to the shadow, the Word to the voice, the express image to the type."[21] It is the very image of condescension and *kenosis*.

On the other hand, his baptism was, unlike some of the more humble moments of his life, a big deal, grand, and glorious. For as the Synoptic Gospels describe, on the day of his baptism the

19. Against the notion that John's message was something novel, the prophetic call to repentance is as ancient as Isaiah's call to "wash yourselves; make yourselves clean; remove the evil of your doings from my eyes; cease to do evil" (Isa 1:16).

20. I once heard of a man who, when asked where he went to church, said, "I am currently practicing my baptism at St. Leo's." The language helpfully implies a progressive movement toward something that has not yet been fully attained, thus requiring steady vigilance lest the gift be neglected, and the goal imperiled.

21. Quoted in Ferguson, *Baptism in the Early Church*, 745, citing *Homily 7* of Theodotus of Ancyra in *Codex Parisianus* gr. 1171 (tenth century), ff. 240r–245r.

heavens were opened and from them the divine voice issued a word of affection ("beloved"), a word of identity ("my son"), and a word of pleasure ("in whom I am well pleased").[22] As the voice of God spoke from the heavens at Jesus' baptism, it is significant to notice that it was not his proper name that was used, but rather his relationship to the Father that was expressed: "[T]his is my beloved *Son, . . .* " The Letter to the Hebrews reflects this priority of identity by referring to the relational "Son" in chapter 1, the name "Jesus" in chapter 2, and the title "Christ" in chapter 3. Baptism is primarily about the celebration of this restored son and daughter relationship to the Father.[23]

Moreover, the paternal pleasure God expressed for all to hear *preceded* Jesus' ministry, rather than being a *response* to it. This chronology is essential to notice in order to avoid any transactional associations with the event. In other words, baptism is not given in exchange or as a reward for righteousness, but as a gift that is prompted by the pure delight God takes in his children, a grace that then propels people to priestly and prophetic roles in the kingdom.

A fourth-century sermon by Ephrem of Syria suggests the important relationship between the baptism administered by John to the people in general, and to Jesus in particular.

> John had been whitening the stains of debt with common water, so that bodies would be fit for the robe of the Spirit imparted by our Lord. Therefore, since the Spirit was with the Son, he came to receive baptism from John to mix the Spirit, which cannot be seen, with water, which can be seen, so that those whose bodies feel the wetness of the water should be aware of the gift of the Spirit in their souls, and that as the outside of the body

22. Cf. Matt 3:17 // Mark 1:11 // and Luke 3:22.

23. Similarly, we see this emphasis on relationship over name (or even role) in the burning bush episode. When Moses asked God, "Who am I that I should go to Pharaoh?" God responded, "I will be with you" (Exod 3:11). It is that divine companionship with people that provides and insures their fundamental identity.

becomes aware of water flowing over it, the inside of the
soul should become aware of the Spirit flowing over it.[24]

In addition to dignifying water (thereby also sanctifying those who
are bathed in it), and establishing the necessity of the sacrament,
Ephrem—who is here typical of patristic theology—demonstrates
the evolution of salvation from the lesser to the greater. While
John merely used plain water, Jesus added the Holy Spirit. Just so,
John, by his own testimony had to decrease, so that Jesus could
increase (cf. John 3:30). Amazingly, Jesus later went on to declare
that "whoever believes in me will do the works I have been doing,
and they will do *even greater things* than these, because I am going
to the Father" (John 14:12; NIV, italics mine).

Perhaps the most significant thing about Jesus' own baptism
has been suggested by Cyril of Alexandria, whose fifth-century
comments on the event are among the longest of the church fathers. With his primary focus not on the baptism itself, but on the
descent of the Spirit, Cyril points to the role of *ruach* in Genesis
2:7, when the Spirit of God breathed the life of God into Adam,
animating the man of dust, rousing him for a vocation of garden-
ing. It is, of course, that same Spirit who rested on Jesus at his
baptism, the very same Spirit who resides in those who are subsequently baptized in his name. This emphasis honors the important
connection made to Nicodemus one night when Jesus insisted
that "no one can enter the kingdom of God without being born of
water and Spirit" (John 3:5). Becoming like Christ is to behave like
him: wet and winded.

Baptism is the means by which people are able to fully participate in the incarnation—the life, death, and resurrection of Jesus. As Keating summarizes, "For Cyril, the recovery of the divine
image in us is not simply the recasting of our deformed nature;
it necessarily involves the reacquisition of the divine life through
the Spirit which was given in the original creation."[25] The baptism
of Jesus, in other words, signals the reentry of the creator into the

24. Ferguson, *Baptism in the Early Church*, 503.

25. Keating, *The Appropriation of the Divine Life in Cyril of Alexandria*,
24–25.

disordered garden, beginning the work of recapitulation. By implication, baptism is the sacramental way we enter into solidarity with the master gardener, and his summons for all who follow him to tend the garden of this world he is presently recreating through the Holy Spirit. "The baptism of Jesus, therefore, was a sign, revealing that 'the reacquisition of the Spirit' meant 'the sanctification of the human race in Christ.'"[26]

This sign of God-with-us, given to the world at the baptism of our Lord, relates to other signs that accompanied his life. While Jesus was still bedewed from the embryonic fluids of his mother's womb, shepherds were alerted to his birth by a unique sign: "[Y]ou will find a child wrapped in bands of cloth and lying in a manger" (Luke 2:12). Moreover, on the day that Jesus was first brought to Jerusalem an old man named Simeon blessed Jesus and then told Mary and Joseph that their "child is destined for the falling and the rising of many in Israel, and to be a sign that will be opposed" (Luke 2:35). Even the way he died was significant. According to Mark, immediately after Jesus took his last breath a centurion said, "Truly this man was God's Son!" (Mark 15:39). In other words, signs were associated with Jesus' life from beginning to end, from his life until his death. However, the preeminent sign was the presence of the Holy Spirit accompanying Jesus throughout his ministry. For just as the Father gave the Spirit to Jesus at his baptism, so Jesus commended his spirit back into the hands of the Father at his crucifixion (cf. Luke 23:46).

Perhaps no sign was more universal and enduring than when Jesus pointed toward water. Throughout the gospel, Jesus can be heard issuing a number of wet invitations: "Very truly, I tell you, no one can enter the kingdom of God without being born of water and Spirit" (John 3:5).[27] It is not likely a coincidence that when Jesus gave instructions to the disciples for their Passover preparations, the singular sign he gave them was to find a man in the city carrying a jar of water (Mark 14:13). Moreover, on the last day of the festival, the so-called "great day," Jesus cried out, "Let anyone

26. Ferguson, *Baptism in the Early Church*, 689.

27. This is the most commonly used baptismal text in the second century.

who is thirsty come to me, and let the one who believes in me drink. As the Scripture has said, 'Out of the believer's heart shall flow rivers of living water'" (John 7:37–38).[28]

While our best manuscripts don't include the (likely legendary) detail about an angel of the Lord stirring up the water adjacent to Jerusalem's Sheep Gate, so that whoever was first in the pool would be healed (John 5:4), it does offer a noteworthy theological insight that some scribe wanted us to see. Perhaps the intention was to help us make a semiotic connection back to the *mayim* of Genesis chapter 1, a word that, significantly, is founded on a Hebrew root with the meaning "to agitate," or "to make an uproar," suggestive of the discomfiting demands baptism makes on a person's life. More vigorous than vapid, the waters of baptism usher people into lifestyles that engage both the struggle against evil, as well as the demands of love—a life that Jesus demonstrated courageously and beautifully, while hardly comfortably.

Paul: Signs of the New Creation

Paul, a man of passion and extremes, represents one of the more compelling and dramatic personal stories of just such a new life in Christ. Indeed, it could be said that he incarnated the drama of a conversion from enemy of God to friend of God. The turning point occurred for him on the road to Damascus as he was en route to incarcerate some Christians as part of his zealous mission to destroy the fledgling church (Acts 9:1–30).

Saul (as he was first known) spent three days in darkness following his blinding encounter with Jesus, who intercepted him and foiled his plans. During those dark days, Luke tells us, he did not eat or drink. Significantly, following those three days of deprivation, when no light, no food, and no water entered his body, and after Ananias laid hands on him to restore his sight, the first thing that Paul did was not to drink or eat. The foremost order of business was to be baptized. This, I suggest, was the pivotal moment

28. Zechariah 14:8, with its reference to "living waters" may be the text Jesus is referring to, although it is far from a direct quote.

in the apostle's life. Far more than something merely symbolic or cosmetic, Paul's baptism encapsulated a change in his mind, a change in his heart, a life-change and a name-change that involved a tectonic shift in identity and purpose. His previous identity and mission as persecutor was completely antithetical to God's purposes. Only after his baptism was his life mission resynchronized by the Holy Spirit, and set on a new course, with a new name, a new identity, and a holy purpose. When doubts or fear crept into his thoughts in the years ahead, that baptismal event most certainly was the anchor point to which he reestablished his moorings, giving him the strength to endure beatings, stoning, imprisonments, and shipwreck (2 Cor 11:23–28).

Influenced by his experience of blinding and seeing, darkness and light, death and life, the Apostle Paul's unique contribution to baptismal identity comes to us through his emphasis on *dying* and *rising* with Christ. I will illustrate this with two examples.

First, in his letter to the Galatians, Paul wrote personally, as one who had integrated the comprehensive effects of baptism: "I have been crucified with Christ; and it is no longer I who live, but it is Christ who lives in me. And the life I now live in the flesh I live by faith in the Son of God, who loved me and gave himself for me" (3:20). Similarly, in his letter to the Romans he posed this most penetrating of rhetorical questions:

> Do you not know that all of us who have been baptized into Christ Jesus were baptized into his death? Therefore we have been buried with him by baptism into death, so that, just as Christ was raised from the dead by the glory of the Father, so we too might walk in newness of life. For if we have been united with him in a death like his, we will certainly be united with him in a resurrection like his. (Rom 6:3–5)

In both examples, the juxtaposition of life and death is lifted up as the central, crucible focal point of the Christian life. A baptism into the life of Jesus requires following the way of the cross, becoming dead to sin as the necessary and ongoing prerequisite to becoming alive to Christ. A great deal of Scripture needs to be overlooked or misinterpreted if one is to miss this emphasis on self-renunciation and the death of the self. The waters of baptism are lethal before they are lifegiving.

Perhaps no other book in the Bible lends itself to being a text for baptismal theology better than the letter to the Ephesians. Although the word occurs only once (4:5), the letter is saturated, so to speak, with the concept of baptism. Perhaps most representative is the author's doxological gush of a prayer: "I pray that you may have the power to comprehend, with all the saints, what is the breadth and length and height and depth (Gk: *Bathos*), and to know the love of Christ that surpasses knowledge, so that you may be filled with all the fullness of God" (Eph 3:18–19). It's not hard to imagine St. Paul[29] here working out of an expansive, sacramental perspective as he prays for the Ephesians, probing the fathoms of baptismal identity. *Bathos*, by the way, is the same word that Luke uses when Jesus instructed Simon Peter to "put out into the *deep water* and let down your nets for a catch" (5:4), and it may well be that the apostle had the Sea of Galilee in mind as a container of thirty-three fathoms of water. Living out of the depth of God's love, it could be said, is akin to taking a "bath": it invites us to go to the deep end of the baptismal pool.

Second, Paul made a similar gush of praise over the blessed mysteries of God in his letter to the Romans: "O the depth [*bathos*] of the riches and wisdom and knowledge of God! How unsearchable are his judgments and how inscrutable his ways!" (11:33). And so, while the literal use of the word fathom occurs only in the Acts of the Apostles (27:28), its metaphorical meaning referring to the depth and richness of God's gifts appears throughout the Bible, springing up and out, I would suggest, from the primal *tehōm* of Genesis.

To find a more figurative and enticing use of the word one need only consult the deuterocanonical book of Sirach, which says, "[N]or is it possible to *fathom* the wonders of the Lord" (18:6).

---

29. While the majority of mainline biblical scholars today dispute Pauline authorship, I attribute the book to him, nonetheless, in the spirit of apostolic authority.

And again, "The first man did not know wisdom fully, nor will the last one *fathom* her. For her thoughts are more abundant than the sea, and her counsel deeper than the great abyss" (24:28–29; italics mine). The Greek word (*orguia*) used here literally means "a stretch of the arms," and so it would seem that in his letter to the Ephesians, the apostle is implicitly referring to baptismal living as he calls the saints to grow up in Christ—that lifelong process of "stretching" from the person we are to the person who is being formed in us. Moreover, as bodies tend to stiffen with age and with inactivity, the baptismal movements of turning from sin and turning toward Jesus are what keep people flexible, limber, and healthy. This exercise of faith is what increases resiliency, and builds capacity for righteousness.

Acts of the Apostles: Signs of the Kingdom

Continuing where John the Baptist ended, and in direct obedience to Jesus' commission, the apostles regularly called people to be baptized as the primary sign of their new life in Christ. Predictably, the two dominant forms of the word ("baptism" and "baptized") occur twenty-six times in Acts, more than any other biblical book.

Beginning with Pentecost—once the wind, the fire, and the chorus of many languages had quieted down—the apostles were faced with the ultimate existential question posed by the crowd that day: "What should we do"? From that decisive moment, the early church issued a consistent apostolic invitation to "be baptized every one of you in the name of Jesus Christ" (2:38). Subsequently, from Simon and the Samarians (8:12–13), to the Ethiopian eunuch (8:37), to Saul in Damascus (9:18), to Cornelius and company (10:48), to Lydia and her household (16:15), to the jailer and his household (16:33), to Crispus and his household (18:8) people, in the various conditions of their lives, responded to the good news and their reception of the Holy Spirit by the simple act of baptism. More than anything else, this was the sign that marked them as God's new creation, and set them on the path to a new way of life.

Peter: Sign of Salvation

Finally, both of the epistles attributed to Peter pick up on the sign language of baptism. Comparing the salvific act of Christ to Noah's ark and the eight people who were saved through the water, Peter writes, "And baptism, which this prefigured, now saves you—not as a removal of dirt from the body, but as an appeal to God for a good conscience, through the resurrection of Jesus Christ" (1 Pet 3:21). Further alluding to both the creative and the destructive forces characteristic of water, the apostle points again to the power of baptism when he writes "that by the word of God heavens existed long ago and an earth was formed out of water and by means of water, through which the world of that time was deluged with water and perished" (2 Pet 3:5–6). In other words, just as Noah and his crew were saved *from* the water *by* the water, the baptized experience similar double-sided effects through regeneration: becoming increasingly dead to sin, and becoming ever more alive to Christ.

Just as the start of the Bible begins on a wet word, so does its finale. "Let everyone who is thirsty come. Let anyone who wishes take the water of life as a gift" (Rev 22:17). However, it is not just the word itself, but the very sound of it that is wet. The voice of Jesus himself gargles the good news: ". . . his voice was like the sound of many waters" (cf. Rev 1:15, 14:2, and 19:6), making the methodology resonate with the meaning. There is moisture in the message, quenching the soul of thirsty Adam.

From Genesis to Revelation, from our beginnings to our endings, God is making all things new through the agency of water. This, the most prevalent resource on the planet, covering approximately 70 percent of the globe, is the sign by which God is reconstituting souls, rehydrating lives for abundance. The biblical texts, in both explicit and tacit ways, witness to how baptism, as a promisign of the suffusion of grace, is operative for disciples of Christ in the ongoing story of salvation.

As if to condense the whole of Scripture in this regard, the writer to the Hebrews, calling his readers to a life of steady discipleship, encourages us to "approach (God) with a true heart in full assurance of faith, with our *hearts sprinkled clean from an evil conscience and our bodies washed with pure water*" (Heb 10:22). This rather holistic allusion to baptismal identity summarizes the dynamic aspects of remaining wet in the living waters, while inhabiting a dry land, by both embracing and enacting the promisign of the new covenant. Said yet another way, (re)turning is the basic movement of discipleship: turning *from*, and turning *toward*. The turning points are *sin* and *savior*, respectively. This is the metanoic "edge" of the baptismal coin. Honoring one's baptism, by following those sacramental signs, takes a lifetime of practice in the holy progression from beginning to becoming. The early church, plentiful with examples of how this was done, is the historical environment to which we now turn our attention.

4

Sacramental Semiotics: Sacred Signs

Here a people of godly race are born for heaven;
the Spirit gives them life in the fertile waters.
The Church-Mother, in these waves, bears her children
like virginal fruit she has conceived by the Holy Spirit.

Hope for the kingdom of heaven, you who are reborn in this spring,
for those who are born but once have no share in the life of blessedness.
Here is to be found the source of life, which washes the whole universe,
Which gushed from the wound of Christ.

Sinner, plunge into the sacred fountain to wash away your sin.
The water receives the old man, and in his place makes the new
man to rise.
You wish to become innocent; cleanse yourself in this bath,
whatever your burden may be, Adam's sin or your own.

There is no difference between those who are reborn; they are one,
in a single baptism, a single Spirit, a single faith.
Let none be afraid of the number of the weight of their sins:
those who are born of this stream will be made holy.

—Lateran basilica, known as the *Inscription of*
Sixtus III (432–440)

LIKE MANY PROTESTANTS, MY theological training drew heavily from the Reformed tradition, a five-hundred-year-old inheritance for which I remain deeply grateful. Reformed theology, however, is a product of its environment, and because the sixteenth-century Reformation was largely a reaction to both errors and abuses in medieval theology and practice, I have been interested in reaching further back, getting reacquainted with some of the early church fathers in order to recover a foundational understanding of the meaning and practice of baptism in the early church, and as a way of correcting for sacramental *drift*. This is not to say that the patristic era necessarily contained the best sacramental theology. Ancient worldviews resulted in biblical perspectives that were often less than accurate, and there are some instructions that, therefore, need to be modified, if not outright rejected. Nonetheless, many of the reflections that endure from that period of church history[1] contain profound theological insights that can be redacted for a postmodern audience. My goal is to recover some of the "lost and neglected materials from the tradition, and thus to reanimate doctrinal reflection both imaginatively and spiritually."[2] The church fathers had superb semiotic imaginations, making intertextual connections that span the canon of Scripture.

This chapter will explore some of the important ways the early church understood the sacrament of baptism, and how the church of today can "rekindle the gift of God" (2 Tim 1:6) for the edification of the body of Christ. Because of the non-transactional nature of baptism, the language of "stewardship" will be interspersed as a reminder of what is gratefully received, and carefully lived by trustees of this gift of grace. Moreover, the relationship between beginning and becoming will be further developed through a variety of patristic lenses.

1. While there is no widespread agreement among scholars, for the purposes of this study I take the patristic period to refer generally to that time in Christian history from the end of the apostolic age to the Council of Chalcedon (451). I do, however, include some of the later writers—like Gregory the Great, for example—whose orthodox influence extended into the early seventh century in the same spirit as the fathers.

2. Coakley, *God, Sexuality, and the Self*, back cover.

As the timeless and enduring sign of a person's constantly new and continually renewing identity in Christ, baptism is the dominant sacramental symbol of a covenant life with God. It is about both beginning and becoming, both preserving and persevering, and as such spans the continuum of a lifetime. As an evangelist, I have come to appreciate the way baptism signals a decision to follow Jesus, and initially marks a person's entrance into the kingdom. As a village pastor, I am growing in my appreciation for the ways baptism gives individuals the sacred identity needed for meaningful discipleship. Moreover, I believe it is the best sacramental container in and out of which to form congregations as the body of Christ. We will proceed around the fraternal twin themes of beginning and becoming.

Often referred to as a rite of initiation, baptism is a beginning, or entry point into a life with Christ, joining us to his bride, the church. The biblical language of *covenant* signals this relational beginning. Just as a birth initiates a life, and a wedding initiates a marriage, baptism marks a believer's initiation into a life of discipleship. As with other covenants, it is a rite of passage that is not finished until a person exhales their last breath. Death marks the moment when a life ends, when a marriage is over, when a baptism is complete.

Consider how the final words of Jesus on the cross, "It is finished" (John 19:30), declared the conclusion of the initial words spoken about him from heaven, "This is my beloved Son, with whom I am well pleased" (Matt 3:17). These Father-Son pronouncements represent the bookends of a life of discipleship. At the beginning are the words of the heavenly Father on the occasion of Jesus' baptism in the Jordan, and thus the inauguration of his public ministry. At the end are the words of the earthly Jesus at the time of his crucifixion signaling the completion of his baptism, and therefore the fulfillment of his life and work. The *it* in "it is finished," encompasses this definitive sense of completion of Christ's messianic assignment of launching the kingdom of heaven on earth, as well as the pleasure the Father has in having his Son now sitting at his right hand, mission accomplished.

The Greek verb *baptō* reflects the rich meaning associated with the sacrament of baptism. The basic sense of the word is "to plunge" or "to dip," leading naturally to "to wet." In some cases, the word referred to "plunging a weapon into a person" reflecting its lethal effects. And in other cases it meant "to dye" (as a result of the dipping action). Adding to the depth of its sacramental implications is the way Homer employs the word in *Odyssey*, writing, "and as when a smith dips [*baptē*] a great axe or adze in cold water . . . to temper it."[3] To *get wet*, to *die*, to *dye*, and to be *tempered* are all powerful images of the life-altering changes effected in and through baptism. Playing with the images the word signifies, one could say that a baptized person is one who has been plunged in the waters, participates in Christ's death, is inked with an invisible and indelible tattoo, and is tempered with the resolve of demanding discipleship, including the possibility of martyrdom. All of which prepare and practice people to be citizens in, and heirs to, the kingdom of God.

Augustine wrote of the ways that baptism "conferred an indelible character" much like a tattoo or a brand, marking a person for life as a child of God. This "permanent marker" of baptism provides the reassurance that one's identity in Christ is eternally secure. Such assurance is what emboldens people to explore and risk, renouncing the fears that might otherwise be debilitating for the demands of discipleship.

The way the early church fathers spoke of this rite of initiation into the kingdom, through the church, was varied and creative as they experimented with metaphors to help mine the mysteries of baptism. Emphasizing the baptismal event as signaling the initial entry point into a life of faith, several of the church fathers (Origen, Gregory of Nyssa, and Clement, in particular) evoked images of Israel, both crossing the Red Sea with Moses, and crossing the Jordan River with Joshua as allegories for Christian baptism. Gregory's work, in particular, is worth a closer look.

3. Quoted by Ferguson, *Baptism in the Early Church*, 39, citing Homer, *Odyssey* 9.392.

Clearly a product of the Alexandrian school, and influenced heavily by Philo, Gregory of Nyssa (c. 335–39) saw, in the life of Moses, a metaphor for growing in the spiritual life. Employing an allegorical method of biblical interpretation, Gregory saw many allusions to baptism in the life of Moses. For example, under the threat of death, the infant Moses was "placed in a basket daubed along its joints with slime and pitch,"[4] a reference to the construction materials Noah used in preparation for the Deluge. He later makes the allusion much more explicit. Writing of the moment when the king's daughter came upon the basket at the river's edge, Gregory speaks of Moses being discovered, "when he gave a childlike cry in the ark." Thus, having been *rescued*, additional baptismal images follow, including *adoption* into a new household, a *non-consuming fire* and *divine voice* from the burning bush, and the commission to *release* his countrymen from Egyptian bondage through the parted *waters* of the Red Sea, gaining them entrance to the land of *promise*, eventually becoming their new *home*.[5]

What is significant and instructive is that the Moses story was continually told and retold among the Israelites until it truly became *their* story, even after many generations had passed. The story of the Exodus, in other words, became a living story, reminding people of the ways God acts in covenant-love (as opposed to convenient love) that often involves drastic measures in order to effect salvation. By introducing distinctively Christian terms in the retelling of this old story, Gregory was simply doing what our Jewish ancestors have always done, but re-signing the Exodus story through a distinctively baptismal lens. Thus appropriated, the images become rich and meaningful for people striving to be glad and grateful trustees of baptism.

The "watery passage" provides a compelling metaphor for the ways a person takes that first, fateful step in crossing the threshold from earth to heaven, from sin to salvation, from death to life, from slavery to freedom. Just as the Israelites left Pharaoh

---

4. Gregory of Nyssa, *The Life of Moses*, 33. "Bitumen and pitch" is how the NRSV more accurately translates this phrase in Exod 2:3.

5. Ibid.; italics mine.

behind in Egypt and followed Moses toward the land of Promise through the waters of the sea, so do the baptized abandon the old Adam, leaving behind a life of bondage to sin, as they follow the new Adam across the waters of the Jordan, into the promise of the kingdom of God. It is a sacred, saving crossing; the threshold, in both cases, consisting, not of wood or of stone, but of water.

In his *Mystagogical Catecheses*, Cyril, the fourth-century bishop of Jerusalem, introduced sweeping, covenantal language that describes the baptismal turning point when one must renounce the devil in order to be initially grafted into Christ:

> [W]hen you renounce Satan, you trample underfoot your entire covenant with him, and abrogate your former treaty with Hell. The gates of God's Paradise are open to you, that garden which God planted in the east, and from which our first parent was expelled for his transgression. When you turned from west to east, the region of light, you symbolized this change of allegiance. Then you were told to say: *I believe in the Father, the Son, and the Holy Spirit, and in one baptism of repentance.*[6]

The water of salvation, in other words, is both tomb and womb. Cyril further describes the baptismal beginning by first quoting and then inverting the wisdom of Solomon, saying, "There is a time to be born and a time to die, but the opposite is true in your case—there is a time to die and a time to be born. A single moment achieves both ends, and your begetting was simultaneous with your death."[7]

It could be said, then, that baptism signals a particular moment in a person's life when believers cross that threshold from death to life, from mortality into immortality, initiating them as citizens of the kingdom of heaven. That it is conceived of in covenantal language adds holy gravitas to its dramatic, life-altering implications.

---

6. Cyril of Jerusalem, *Mystagogical Catecheses* 1.9, quoted by Johnson, *The Rites of Christian Initiation*, 123.

7. Ibid., 2.4, quoted by Johnson, *The Rites of Christian Initiation*, 123–24.

However, *the baptismal event itself no more completes a person for a life of faith than does a wedding day complete a couple for marriage.* In both cases, it is the beginning point of a covenantal relationship that then gets practiced and worked out for the rest of one's life. As Tertullian famously said, "Christians are made, not born."[8] Such a holy identity involves daily practices that, over a lifetime, form people for the royal priesthood (cf. 1 Pet 2:9). Baptismal identity, I suggest, is the foundational distinctive by which people are formed, providing a sacred *ego* or what might better be described as a *thego*[9] out of which to live.

While baptism has typically been understood as a rite of initiation into the household of God, its richness lies in the new identity it conveys to people, providing new meaning, new purpose, and new direction for their lives. In other words, baptism affords a dynamic identity for discipleship, providing a sacred cosmology out of which to live, by prompting the continual, daily choices of renunciation and affirmation: turning from sin and turning toward Christ. These are the holy *noes* and *yeses* of our lives. However, for baptism to be a potent source for human telos it must be understood less as a one-time life event, and more as a life*style*, one that is pursued and preserved through mindfulness, intention, and discipline.

In his magisterial book, Everett Ferguson, one of our preeminent patristics scholars, gives us access and insight into how the fathers championed a dynamic understanding of the sacrament. If catechesis is the instructional period designed to prepare a person for baptism, mystagogy is the practice of living it. Following are some of the more notable representative samples of how the fathers encouraged people to plunge the depths of their baptismal identity.

8. Tertullian, *Apologeticus pro Christianis* 18.4.

9. This is a portmanteau of my creation combining the Greek word *Theos* and the Latin word *Ego*, resulting in a "godly self," or that process of becoming holy, conceptually similar to the Eastern Orthodox notion of *Theosis*. Additionally, Augustine, in one of his sermons, encouraged the newly baptized to "become who you are" (Sermon 272).

As early as the second-century sermon of II Clement we see this emphasis of continually honoring the gift of baptism through lifestyle choices. "With what confidence shall we enter into the royal house of God if we do not *keep our baptism* pure and undefiled? Or who will be our advocate if we are not found to have holy and righteous works?"[10]

Similarly, the third-century *The Questions of Bartholomew* (likely based on the original *Gospel of Bartholomew*) supposedly—but dubiously—quotes Jesus saying, "It is good if he who is baptized *preserves his baptism* without blame."[11]

Again, the *Acts of Paul* contains this sense of preservationist language (although some scholars believe it was referring more specifically to maintaining celibacy), saying, "Blessed are they who have *kept their baptism secure*, for they shall rest with the Father and the Son."[12]

In one of his more noteworthy sermons, Chromatius of Aquileia speaks of the need for the recipients of baptism—because it is given only once—to preserve it from sin. "Watch so that you do not return to your former sins and incur danger of death, because the grace of baptism is given only once."[13]

Even Origen employs this sense of honoring the historic baptismal event with his use of past-tense language. In his *Homilies on Luke*, commenting about the need for a baptism by fire, he nonetheless references water baptism when he writes, "For, it is fitting that one should be baptized first in 'water and the Spirit.' Then, when he comes to the fiery river, he can show that he *preserved the bathing* in water and the Spirit."[14]

In all of these examples, the references contain what might be referred to as distinctively *maintenance* language, with an accompanying sense of preservation. From the perspective of stewardship, then, it appears that these writers are representative of

10. Quoted in Ferguson, *Baptism in the Early Church,* 207; italics mine.

11. Quoted in ibid., 227; italics mine.

12. Quoted in ibid., 229; italics mine.

13. Quoted in ibid., 660.

14. Quoted in ibid., 409; italics mine.

a conservative approach, keeping and holding intact this sacred gift, much like the one-talent servant in a parable Jesus once told designed to contrast the ways that people can exercise the gifts they have been given and entrusted by God (cf. Matt 25:14–30). In other words, these are perspectives that emphasize *beginnings*, or the entry point to a covenantal life of faith. As important a beginning as baptism is, it is not enough. When it comes to *exercising* the gift of baptism, where are the entrepreneurial two- and five-talent servants? Who is showing us the way of *becoming*?

The Apologist Justin Martyr leads the way. Summarizing his view of baptism in his introduction to the Lord's Supper, Justin plants one foot in past-tense language to reflect an emphasis on the sacramental deed that was done, and then he places his other foot in the present, providing a bridge from the historical event to a present-day lifestyle, writing, "This food is called by us eucharist, of which no one is allowed to partake except the one who believes the things taught by us to be true, *was washed* in the bath for forgiveness of sins and regeneration, and *who lives* in the manner Christ taught."[15] In commenting on this excerpt, Ferguson makes the helpful observation that the object of faith being suggested by Justin is not in the life of Christ himself, but in Christian teachings.

It is left mostly to Tertullian to introduce somewhat playful images that encourage people to *live* their baptisms. Much like the multitalented servants who creatively put their gifts to use, Tertullian is a champion in the art of swimming in the baptismal waters, to actively experience and to actually enjoy the abundance of the kingdom on earth as it is in heaven. It is significant that the first word in his exordium on the subject begins on the unmistakable note of joy: "Happy is our sacrament of water, in that, by washing away the sins of our early blindness, we are set free and admitted into eternal life!"[16]

So great is Tertullian's delight in this gift that he continues by introducing additional playful images. Consider the following wonderful, pastoral encouragement: "But we, little fishes, after the

15. Quoted in ibid., 242; italics mine.
16. Tertullian, *On Baptism* 3.

example of our ICTHUS Jesus Christ, are born in water, nor have we safety in any other way than by permanently abiding in water."[17] The image, of course, encourages people to think of themselves as theologically amphibious such that those who become dry eventually die. We need to stay immersed and moist (a word Tertullian is fond of, along with "juicy"), splashing in the baptismal waters, staying in proximity to the fount of life not only in order to stay alive but also in order for our existence to be truly lively. Water was so pervasive an image in the early church that Tertullian called Christianity a *religio aqae.*

By contrast, Tertullian speaks of the dangers lurking about in "arid" environments where snakes are known to live, tempting us, through a variety of seductions, to abandon the life-giving waters, leading us to death. Tertullian, a master at making semiotic connections between the two testaments of the Bible, was alluding, of course, to the craftiness of the serpent who tricked Adam into breaking faith with God (cf. Gen 3:1), as the same snake who shows up among the sons and daughters of Adam today, tempting us to stray from both the demands and the delights of the new covenant. Elsewhere, in his treatise *On Repentance,* he emphasizes this sense of holy vigilance when it comes to being trustees of baptism, since there are compelling forces that are competing for our souls, and he therefore issues, "a strong message about living above sin after baptism."[18]

As another example of his semiotic skill, Tertullian elsewhere speaks of the Holy Spirit, who hovered over the waters of creation, as the same Spirit who "would continue to linger over the waters of the baptized."[19] Following his lead, one could metaphorically attribute a brooding nature to that same hovering Spirit, an image evocative of poultry. Laying hens sometimes get broody, providing warmth to their incubating eggs, waiting for new life to crack open from beneath them. Normally curious and active, scratching for worms and chasing down bugs, brooding chickens

17. Ibid.

18 Ferguson, *Baptism in the Early Church,* 348.

19. Tertullian, *On Baptism,* 7.

are—trance-like—singularly focused, as if they have nothing else to do, nowhere to go. The image of the brooding Spirit, hovering over the chaotic waters of the inchoate creation, can be appropriated for how that same Holy Spirit hovers over the baptismal waters of the new creation, and then can be found tenaciously brooding over the baptized, whose souls are incubating in the watery womb of new birth.

Not surprisingly, Tertullian wasn't the lone voice for lifestyle baptism rising above the otherwise large preserve of sacramental theology. The work of Origen provides yet another example of how the early church encouraged people to become what they were baptized to be. Commenting on the Letter of Paul to the Romans, Origen insists on the necessity of a vital, lively baptism, writing, "For you must not imagine that the renewing of the life, which is said to have been done once, suffices. On the contrary *at all times and daily*, this newness must, if it can be said, be renewed."[20] In fact, Origen consistently emphasized his expectations for the moral and spiritual life of the ones who had been baptized.

Closely resembling this emphasis on the implications of baptism for morality, and as an agent of transformation toward a godly lifestyle, Gregory of Nyssa referred to the grace of God contained in the sacramental waters as propelling people "to grow into perfect maturity." Such growth is necessary since "[b]aptism destroys sins but not the inclination to them."[21] Likewise, in the *Shepherd*, Hermas addresses the expectation that stewards of the gift of baptism, having "received the forgiveness of sins ought no longer to continue in sin but to live in purity."[22]

Keenly aware of the moral requirements assumed in the baptized, Augustine argued for the catechesis of baptismal candidates to include not only what to believe but also how to live. Augustine understood baptism as the beginning point from which all other virtues of discipleship—or *becoming* Christian—flowed, especially prayer, which daily renews one's baptismal identity and rejuvenates

20. Quoted in Ferguson, *Baptism in the Early Church*, 414; italics mine.
21. Quoted in ibid., 616.
22. Quoted in ibid., 216.

one's baptismal practices. Similarly, Chrysostom, in his *Baptismal Instructions*, in referring to the baptized, writes, "they not only are cleansed but *become* holy, too, and just."[23] One of Chrysostom's favorite baptismal images was that of marriage. Addressing the catechumens in his care he was fond of telling them, "Behold, . . . the days of your spiritual marriage are close at hand."[24]

A much lesser-known description of baptism as it informs and affects one's lifestyle is found in a homily by Proclus, bishop of Constantinople (434–446). Addressing his catechumens by reminding them of their new identity in Christ, he went on to describe how they must henceforth live. Referring to their baptismal vows, he urged them, "This you called out in words. Demonstrate it with your deeds! Sanction your confession with your conduct . . . Do not return to the place whence you ran away." Finally, he reminded them that the devil is the "enemy from whom you have fled."[25]

In an earlier sermon, Proclus makes an even more explicit reference to the kind of person baptism leads us to grow into, inspiring his listeners to:

> Become immortal in virtue.
>
> Become a genuine son with a view to righteousness.
>
> Become a perpetual king.
>
> Become an undefiled bridegroom.
>
> Be radiant without stain.[26]

"Becoming" is distinctively hopeful language, a reminder that we are on a progressive journey toward holiness. Baptism moves us continually closer to Christ, forming us to become more fully like Christ, "from one degree of glory to another" (2 Cor 3:18).

Taken as a whole then, it is evident that the Fathers recognized that one of the gifts of baptism was to provide people with

23. Quoted in ibid., 549; italics mine.
24. Quoted in ibid., 548.
25. Quoted in ibid., 749.
26. Quoted in ibid., 752.

a way to imagine themselves living on the *wet edge*[27] of their baptismal identity, participating in their new life in Christ, and cooperating with the Spirit who is sanctifying them to be more Christ-like. Whatever the images one chooses to use, they are most appropriate when they favor movement or growth over *status quo*, or that progression from *beginners* to *becomers*. That movement, according to the patristic tradition, requires daily turning from sin and turning toward Jesus. This *metanoic* movement reflects the ongoing rhythms of baptism, represented by the continual invitation to turn, and it invites us to re-turn to the lethal, lifegiving waters of the no and yes of discipleship: the obliteration of the old self, as prerequisite for the maturation of the new. We are always turning as we repeatedly return to the font: the fount of life.

Baptism is the propellant that thrusts us meaningfully into the world. Just as the Spirit drove Jesus into the wilderness immediately following his baptism, we are sent into the world. Just as Jesus faced a series of temptations from the devil, we confront the evils of our environment. And just as Jesus was forced to renounce Satan in order to accomplish the will of the Father, so we too practice the behaviors of turning from sin (no!), and turning to God (yes!). Baptism drives and decides.

At one level, then, baptism reflects the simplicity of wisdom contained in a primitive first-century book known as *The Didache* ("The Teaching"), which famously posits the two ways: "A Way of Life and a Way of Death, and the difference between the two Ways is great."[28] The essence of this ancient teaching closely reflects both the wisdom literature of the Old Testament (Proverbs in particular), and New Testament exhortations (especially those found in the Sermon on the Mount). To the ears of modern-day Christians, it can sound surprisingly basic in content, beginning with the commands to love God and to love others as the path that leads to life.

---

27. The intended image here is that of maintaining a wet edge when painting so that the finish is smooth, without ridges.

28. Quoted in Staniforth, trans., *The Apostolic Fathers*, 191.

According to *The Didache*, the road to death, as one would expect, is characterized by evil and includes a long laundry list of sins, most of which appear in the Scriptures (such as adultery, fornication, greed, slander, etc.). Additionally, this teaching issues a grave warning when it comes to neglecting the poor. For example, the way of death is represented by those people who are "without pity for the poor or feeling for the distressed . . . they turn away the needy and oppress the afflicted; they aid and abet the rich but arbitrarily condemn the poor; they are utterly and altogether sunk in iniquity. Flee, my children, from all this!"[29] The beauty of simplifying the complexities of life as a choice between two ways reflects the baptismal movements of turning from sin and turning toward Christ—the renunciations and the affirmations of a living faith.

The stewardship of this sacred lifestyle, located in the richness of baptismal images, requires both the care and the exercise of the covenant, reflective of both beginning in the life of Christ and becoming more like Christ. However, as followers of the Way have long known, spiritual challenges persist long after baptism; among us and within us are saboteurs to sanctification.

Recognizing the ongoing temptations to sin, as well as the reality of actually falling into sin, thereby dishonoring the covenant, the early church found language that was useful in restoring a person who had strayed from their baptismal moorings. Acknowledging the need for ongoing repentance subsequent to baptism, and correcting for drift for those who had gotten off-course, several of the fathers introduced the notion of the "second plank." Thomas Aquinas (1225–1247) gives credit to Jerome (c.347–420) for the term where he refers to penitence as "a plank for those who have had the misfortune to be shipwrecked."

However, the phrase "second plank" is originally attributable to Tertullian, who rather poetically describes the grace of having our baptismal identity restored through the act of repentance. In chapter 4 of *On Repentance* he writes,

---

29. *Didache* (trans. Staniforth, 191).

To all sins, then, committed whether by flesh or spirit, whether by deed or will, the same *God* who has destined penalty by means of judgment, has withal engaged to grant pardon by means of repentance, saying to the people, "Repent thee, and I will save thee;" and again, "I live, saith the Lord, and I will (have) repentance rather than death." Repentance, then, is "life," since it is preferred to "death." That repentance, O sinner, like myself (nay, rather, less than myself, for pre-eminence in sins I acknowledge to be mine), do you so hasten to, so embrace, as a shipwrecked man the protection of some plank. This will draw you forth when sunk in the waves of sins, and will bear you forward into the port of the divine clemency. Seize the opportunity of unexpected felicity: that you, who sometime were in God's sight nothing but "a drop of a bucket," and "dust of the threshing-floor," and "a potter's vessel," may thenceforward become that "tree" which is sown beside the waters, is perennial in leaves, bears fruit at its own time, and shall not see fire, nor "axe." Having found "the truth," repent of errors; repent of having loved what God loves not: even we ourselves do not permit our slave-lads not to hate the things which are offensive to us; for the principle of voluntary obedience consists in similarity of minds.[30]

Problematically, even with so lavish a description of grace, Tertullian maintained a rigorist interpretation of the troubling text of Hebrews 6:4–6,[31] and insisted that there can be no reconciliation for a person having committed a postbaptismal sin. Attempting to

---

30. Tertullian, *On Repentance,* 4 (trans. Thelwall, *ANF* 3:659–60); in "The Tertullian Project," accessed October 21, 2013. http://www.tertullian.org/anf/anf03/footnote/fn113.htm#P11305_3204867.

31. "For it is impossible to restore again to repentance those who have been enlightened, and have tasted the heavenly gift, and have shared in the Holy Spirit, and have tasted the goodness of the word of God and the powers of the age to come, and then have fallen away, since on their own they are crucifying again the Son of God and are holding him up to contempt" (Heb 6:4–6). Similar passages in this letter that raise questions about the doctrine of eternal security are found in 10:26–31 and 12:17.

reconcile these apparently conflicting positions, F. F. Bruce posits that

> Tertullian had one particular kind of sin in mind, and one which actually does not enter into our author's argument here: according to Tertullian, the writer of this warning passage (identified by him with Barnabas), "who learnt this *from* apostles, and taught it *with* apostles, never knew of any second repentance promised by apostles to the adulterer and fornicator.[32]

Additionally, it may well be that Tertullian, out of his insistence that baptism is a sacred gift, wanted to emphasize the importance of honoring it through lifestyles of holiness. Even so, his notion of the second plank—as a sort of makeshift lifeboat in the stormy sea of sin in which a person has been shipwrecked—remains a compelling image of rescue and forgiveness. While "walking the plank" is now more commonly associated with death by drowning, Tertullian's image of the second plank suggests how repentance is the life preserver that restores sinners to the grace of God's unending mercy. The wet sacrament, of course, captures beautifully both sides of the baptismal coin: the necessity for the old self to be destroyed in order for a new life in Christ to be established.

Echoing and summarizing this spirit of the fathers is Martin Luther's reflection on the nature of one's life in Christ with its vague allusion to baptism:

> This life, therefore, is not godliness but the process of becoming godly, not health, but getting well, not being but becoming, not rest but exercise. We are not now what we shall be, but we are on the way. The process is not yet finished, but it is actively going on. This is not the goal but it is the right road. At present, everything does not gleam and sparkle, but everything is being cleansed.[33]

---

32. Bruce, *The Epistle To The Hebrews*, 123.
33. Luther, *Luther's Works*, 32:24.

As we saw in chapter 2, capitulation to the North American culture has muddied the waters for holy living. What is needed is a way to recover a sacred identity that has been sullied by the values of consumption and production. One way to do that is to return to Irenaeus, with his concept of recapitulation. Generally speaking, the notion of recapitulation is a concept of the atonement whereby the disobedience of Adam is reversed through the obedience of Jesus as the "second Adam," and restores humanity's relationship with God to its prelapsarian condition. The damage done under a Garden tree was undone on the Calvary tree. The continual movements of the baptized to repent of their sin and return to Christ is the lifelong liturgy for becomers.

Although considered to be macabre by many, the images enshrined beneath the Church of *Santa Maria della Concezione dei Cappuccini* in Rome are a startling reminder of every person's eventual fate. There in the famous Capuchin Crypt some years ago, my children and I walked by an assortment of skeletal remains from thousands of monks collected over many years. Some of the bones have been artfully arranged into patterns or made into chandeliers, while others are simply (and apparently irreverently) piled in a heap. Once a visitor gets past the initial shock of being surrounded by so many human remains, it is actually a helpful visual aid, a reminder of the fleeting nature of life, and a powerful motivator to spend their limited days intentionally and with purpose. Reinforcing this reminder are the haunting words inscribed at the far end of the crypt, here in translation from the original Latin:

What you are now we used to be; what we are now you will be.

As we have seen, the early church Christians, in both the East and the West, were exposed to potent images that helped to form their baptismal imaginations in a way that was more dynamic than passive, encouraging active participation in the process of sanctification. Notwithstanding the rigorous demands and expectations that were often imposed as prerequisites for receiving the sacrament, i.e., extensive catechesis, multiple exorcisms, and thorough examinations, the fathers employed images that yet encourage today's faithful to take the plunge and to continue swimming in the baptismal waters, in the lifelong decisions that turn us from death and re-turn us to life. For when we well know both who we are and to whom we belong, we are well on our way to knowing how to well live.

Our baptismal beginning, in other words, results in the ripple effects of who we eventually grow to become for those who remain engaged in the struggle between sin and sanctification from beginning to end. For, as Gregory of Nyssa plainly said, "What you have not become, you are not."[34] Or, as Cyprian of Carthage similarly but more positively suggested, the Christian life involves becoming what one has begun to be: "We pray that we who were sanctified in baptism may be able to persevere in that which we have begun to be."[35]

34. Quoted in Ferguson, *Baptism in the Early Church*, 616; citing *Catechetical Oration* 40, *GNO* 102, 24–103.

35. Quoted in ibid., 361; citing *To Donatus* 5 and 14.

5

Living Wet: Full Immersion
in Abundant Life

Our entire spiritual life is the activation
of the seed planted in baptism.
—St. Mark the Ascetic (sixth century)

The real voyage of discovery consists not in seeking new landscapes,
but in having new eyes.
—Marcel Proust

This you called out in words. Demonstrate it with your deeds!
Sanction your confession with your conduct.
Do not return to the place when you ran away.
—Proclus

THE CONGREGATION I SERVE has given me the nickname "the child whisperer" because I tend to have a calming effect on children. This, however, is not some naturally endowed intrinsic gift. Rather, at the baptisms of infants there are a number of things I do to make it a smooth experience, worthy of baby album photographs. To begin with I always spend some time with the children before their baptismal day so that they become acquainted with my voice, comfortable with my presence. I even practice the "hand off" from the parent to me ahead of time so as to avoid any awkwardness that might incite anxiety in the child. On the morning of the christening day, the font is filled with warm water to reduce the shock, making the experience feel more like a bath.

Fortunately—as it turned out—none of that worked at a recent baptism in our church and, immediately after her baptism, "Evie" started crying and then proceeded to escalate uncontrollably, even after being returned to her mother. "So much for my reputation," I thought to myself. Afterwards, a colleague who was visiting, and who had observed the event, shared with me his recent experience of witnessing a baptism in a Russian Orthodox service where he watched the priest immerse a naked infant three times in a font of cold water. Predictably, the child, after the brief pause of breathless surprise, screamed some of the paint off the ceiling. When speaking to the grandmother of the child after worship, asking if there wasn't a more hospitable way to administer the welcoming sacrament, my friend was startled to hear her say, through her thick Russian accent, "Oh no, if the baby did not cry the priest would pinch him until he did! When babies are first born the best sound to hear is the cry; it means that they are breathing, alive, healthy. Baptism is a birthing!"

My experience with Evie, coupled with the story of the Russian Orthodox baptism, has caused me to rethink the images of my role as a baptizer, now making me want to exchange the nickname "child-whisperer" for "midwife": awakening, even *startling* people to rebirth into a new world and a new life. It is, as the Lutheran song writer, John Ylvisaker, calls it, our "borning cry." The fertility of the birthing image is worth further elaboration as a metaphor for being "born from above" (John 3:3).

After first describing two opposing and extreme styles of leadership—autocratic and laissez faire (highly controlling in the former case, easy-going and permissive in the latter)—a recent handbook to the catechumenate has suggested that a third, or middle way may be more appropriate when it comes to faith formation and the development of disciples. Consider the maieutic way:

> The midwife does not herself give birth, but makes birth easier by providing support, comfort, ideas, direction, encouragement, and strength when needed . . . To participate in the maieutic process . . . is to serve as a midwife, that is, to assist in a birthing process of bringing into the light a new creation . . . The midwife assists the creator to expel from the womb that which has been nurtured, nourished, and warmed into viability. The midwife implants nothing from without and brings only her skill and strength to coach the natural process, albeit a process fraught with danger, labor, and pain.[1]

I find the notion of the role as that of *assistant to the creator* to be a compelling description of what ministers do in companioning people through their lives, being alert to signs of redemption (while not being deterred by the presence and necessity of pain), continually asking the question, "To what new life might this person be giving birth?" Like a lot of things in the modern age, the church has softened some of the startling effects of baptism. Such things as christening gowns, warm water, and climate-controlled sanctuaries may end up having the unintended consequence of creating associations of only comfort and joy, whereas the administration and lifestyle of baptism should provoke images of profound struggle.[2] Like birthing, the transition to a new life in Christ is fraught with discomfort, even pain. In fact, there may be no other event where life and death are in such close proximity to one another than during a birthing. Eliminating shock entirely

---

1. Bushkofsky, *Go Make Disciples*, 63.

2. In a "life, liberty, and the pursuit of happiness" culture, *struggle*, in its many manifestations, may be viewed as an unwelcome intruder, and the very enemy of a meaningful life. Offering a correcting perspective to this false assumption, the Dutch Reformed theologian Berkhof makes a convincing argument to demonstrate how struggle is normative and necessary for progress in the Christian life, as necessitated by the death of the "old man" to make room for the emergence of the "new man." See Berkhof, *Christian Faith*, 512–15.

during the administration of baptism may, paradoxically, result in the development of disciples who become *shocked* when their lives are interrupted by pain, or when facing death.[3] Baptism provides necessary *shock value* to disciples by initiating them into a life in Christ, a life full of rebirthing surprises, both pleasant and painful, yet always good.

Churches that are interested in attracting new people may be prone to methodologies that do not reflect the rigors of *costly discipleship*.[4] Beginnings are important inasmuch as they set a trajectory for a lifetime. If the beginning is wrong, the end result will be wrong as well, along with much that occurs in between. I suggest that much of the present-day malaise in the church of North America is largely the result of adapting methods of evangelism that are more suitable as propaganda techniques for the enterprise of capitalism than for calling people to a holy life as citizens of the kingdom of God. Failure to help people take their first, crucial steps on the road of costly discipleship amounts to a misrepresentation of the gospel and is a disservice to people who desire to live meaningfully in a broken world. While I applaud many of the emerging church efforts that are creatively reaching out to the un-baptized, they may inadvertently create some unexpected results by not more accurately reflecting the *crucible* nature of a life in Christ.

The current cultural (some might even argue *ecclesiastical*) ethos in which we live suffers from a lack of sacramental imagination. Unlike the Ethiopian eunuch, who, upon recognizing Jesus as the Messiah and seeing some water, asked, "Here's water. Why can't I be baptized?" (Acts 8:37; MSG), most people today do not make such automatic associations. Relatively speaking, the church does well at extending invitations to "come to the table," but it needs to be more intentional about the summons to "come to the water."

3. The "rebirth" (Gk: *palingenesias*) through baptismal waters of which Paul writes to Titus (3:5) is best understood as a lifelong process of becoming a new creation, as opposed to a one-time historical event.

4. Bonhoeffer, who coined the term, also wrote that, "when God bids a man he bids him come and die." See Bonhoeffer, *The Cost of Discipleship*, 89.

The purpose of this chapter is to demonstrate how baptismal theology can be integrated with the practice of baptismal lifestyles, largely through sharing the personal stories of individuals and faith communities who are seeking to intentionally embrace lifestyles of living wet.

Is there a way, I want to ask, to return to the baptismal waters, and discover there, not a scum-covered pond littered with liturgical flotsam, but a stream in which flows living water (John 4:10–11), and the very fountain of life (Ps 36:9)?[5] Moreover, how does one bridge the integrative gap between sacramental theology and sacred living? How do people *live* their baptism?

The North American Association of the Catechumenate (NAAC) is pointing the way. Founded in 1995, its mission is to "promote and nurture the catechumenal process in order that the whole faith community might fulfill Christ's commission to make disciples, baptizing and teaching all peoples." Even more compelling is its vision, which has, among other things,

> the goal of helping change congregational culture so that
> faith communities can become lively, faithful minorities
> in a post-Christian, post-modern culture and serve as
> transformational communities of disciples for the sake
> of God's mission in the world.[6]

Intrigued by the concept (which is really a recovery of ancient church practices) I attended a training event held in Vancouver, B.C.[7]

---

5. Elsewhere, the image is similarly used in the context of prophetic accusation to describe the nature of God during a time when the people of Israel "have forsaken me, *the fountain of living water*, and dug cisterns for themselves, cracked cisterns that can hold no water" (Jer 2:13; italics mine). Jeremiah's condemnation is a result of the people exchanging an eternal source of life for inferior ones.

6. North American Association of the Catechumenate, accessed November 5, 2015, http://catechumenate.org/index.php?page=about-us.

7. The day I first stumbled upon this group while doing research months previously, I came home and declared to my wife, "I've found my people!" To be with them for three days was akin to a trekkie being at a Star Trek convention. Not only were they smitten by the power of baptism to shape and renew

The primary pedagogy for introducing us to the catechumenate was to actually practice it. Over a period of three days we worshiped by following the cycles of the liturgical year, each worship experience designed to represent a step in the baptismal journey. We began with a "Rite of Welcome" in which various participants at the conference role-played people who were in the early stages of inquiring into faith. Each was assigned a sponsor who was to continue with them through the process.

Next, in a service reflecting the liturgy of the First Sunday in Lent, the "Rite of Enrollment" was observed, signaling the start of a formal process of catechesis. In the practice of a local congregation, the enrollment would be followed by a period of instruction and exploration around the basics of the faith, in preparation for baptism.

The third service was an Easter Vigil, which included an elaborate candlelight liturgy, culminating in the celebration (or, in this case, *reaffirmation*) of baptisms, and followed by receiving the Eucharist. Afterwards, a festive reception added to the celebrative atmosphere, providing an occasion to welcome the newly baptized.

Interspersed between worship services during those three days were seminars that reflected the actual catechumenate process, providing demonstrations of how it can be taught. For example, Paul Palumbo, a pastor in the ELCA tribe, described how he educates catechumens about the liturgy so they can be more meaningfully formed by it. "Imagine a situation in which you feel completely overwhelmed and out of control," he said, "something you are entirely incapable of managing or resolving. It might be an addiction, a difficult relationship, a health issue. Whatever it is there is no remedy in sight, leaving you feeling altogether helpless." He then suggested that, in the face of such formidable circumstances, there is only one appropriate response, and it is one that is integrated into the weekly Lutheran liturgy during the prayers

---

and redirect lives for the kingdom of God, but many of them were walking encyclopedias of trivia and baptismal information from different periods of church history. I was relieved and pleased to discover other "baptismal nerds" in North America.

of confession, as the congregation sings, *Kyrie Eleison*: Lord, have mercy. When life implodes, when there are no other resources available, these are the words that give voice to hopelessness. Because of the One to whom they are addressed, the One whose "mercies never come to an end" (Lam 3:22), hope endures. More than merely seeking forgiveness for sins, this is the cry for help when life becomes unnavigable, when the best that a shipwrecked person can do is to throw herself on the mercy of God. By practicing this liturgy every Sunday, worshippers gradually become fluent in the language of prayer for the other days of the week as well. *Kyrie Eleison.*

The final worship service reflected the celebration of Pentecost, fifty days after Easter. The catechumenate process refers to this as the "Affirmation of Vocation." I was asked that morning to be among the four participants to assume the part of someone who had been baptized during the Easter Vigil. What I first thought was merely role-playing, ended up impacting me profoundly.

Having had "fifty days" to reflect on it, we were each invited to make a simple statement about how our baptismal identity was to be expressed vocationally. We gathered at the font, and after singing a song, reading some liturgy, and splashing some water, we shared our statements. When it was my turn, without having given it much thought beforehand, I said, "My name is Eric Peterson. I affirm my gift as a writer, and I dedicate myself to use words to the glory of God." After each of our affirmations the assembly sang this response:

> *Blessed be God, who chose you in Christ.*
> *Live in love as Christ loved us.*

The service concluded, we said our goodbyes, and I got in my car to drive home. However, about an hour later, just as I was crossing the international border back into Washington State, I looked in the rearview mirror, with this realization: "I think something may have happened to me back there." As a result, I spent the rest of the seven-hour trip absorbing an identity I had previously resisted, praying for the Holy Spirit to prompt me with what to write.

*Baptismal imagination is the awareness that "something hap-
pened to me back there."* The historical event of baptism spills into
our present and overflows into our future, transporting us on the
sacred stream of meaning and purpose. Spirit-led, it involves first
hearing the invitation that emerges from the depths, and then
heeding the summons to be deepened, as "deep calls to deep" (Ps
42:7).

However, one of the challenges of baptism is that, as a signifi-
er, it does not remain visible, as do most other signs. Once a person
has been baptized, there is no ongoing evidence of having been so
claimed and identified—no uniform, no badge, no title, not even a
faint watermark. At least with the Abrahamic covenant there was
the indelible nature of circumcision, but even that was not readily
visible to more than the most intimate of acquaintances. If baptism were accompanied by something more durable—like getting
a tattoo, or a unique haircut, or a piece of jewelry—it might create
a less precarious reminder of one's identity. We aren't given that.
Quickly after getting splashed in the threefold name we dry off, the
words wisp away, the memory and the meaning of the event then
entrusted to absentminded people, putting baptism in jeopardy of
being overlooked, misunderstood, or even altogether forgotten.

This, I believe, is the crisis of our age. We have forgotten who
we are, because we have forgotten *whose* we are. We need to rekindle memory. We need to be reminded. We need our baptismal
identity to be evoked in order to live out of it, and in order to live
into it. Sponge-like, our lives need to be sacramentally sopped,
absorbing the means of grace that rehydrate arid souls.

Water is essential for life in its beginnings, in its renewings,
and in its endurings. Its beginnings, in which our embryonic formation and development occurs, take place in the dark waters of
the womb. Frederick Buechner, in his inimitable style, reflects on
the significance of water:

> For nine months we breathe in it. The sight of water in
> oceans, rivers, and lakes is soothing to the spirit as al-
> most nothing else. To swim in it is to become as weight-
> less and untrammeled as in dreams. The wake of a ship,

86

the falling of a cataract, and the tumbling of a brook can hold us spellbound for hours, and in times of drought we feel as parched in our being as the lawn that crackles beneath our feet.

Air is our element, but water is our heart's delight. "My flesh faints for thee," the Psalmist sings, "as in a dry and weary land where no water is" (63:1). And among the last things that Jesus ever said, and among the most human, were the words, "I thirst" (John 19:28).[8]

Journeying by stages—from beginning, to becoming, to ending— water is the foundation of life, a delight to the heart. To be removed from it for any length of time is perilous to one's health—thus the need for sacramental memory.

Baptismal Reminders

I have sometimes felt that one of the things I am trying to do in my own ministry context is to conduct a series of experiments to see if the Word made *flesh* can also be the Word made *wet*. It has been my desire to extend and expand baptismal images far beyond the one-time sacrament itself to ones that create a more comprehensive, pervasive sacramental awareness. Get caught in the rain: remember your baptism. Drink a glass of water: remember you are the baptized. Sit in your hot tub: remember. But do more than remember. Such recollection leads to substantive lifestyle choices that involve both the hard work of love and the unpleasant business of dying to self.

While I love words, and believe in their power to transform, I am convinced that they are not, by design, adequate on their own for the life-changing work of salvation and liberation. Yet when they are accompanied by a tangible experience, engaging the senses, captivating the imagination, they can be truly transformative. This, of course, is the wisdom of not uncoupling the important, synergistic partnership of word and sacrament, or words and things.

8. Buechner, *Beyond Words*, 407–8.

To do this I have conducted playful experiments with water in worship, using the font as a focal point. On a recent Sunday, after leading the prayer of confession from the pulpit, I then moved to the baptismal font and raised high a large pitcher of water. As the water was slowly poured into the bowl, splashing delightfully, catching sunlight, I posed the questions asked of anyone about to be baptized, and gave time for a verbal response after each one:

- *Trusting in the gracious mercy of God, do you turn from the ways of sin and renounce evil and its power in the world?* (I do.)

- *Do you turn to Jesus Christ, and accept him as your Lord and Savior, trusting in his grace and love?* (I do.)

- *Will you be Christ's faithful disciple, obeying his Word and showing his love?* (I will, with God's help.)

With the pitcher empty and the font full (indicative of a great and "wonderful exchange" having occurred[9]) I then declared: "You have been washed clean, and renewed in the waters of baptism, adopted forever as the beloved daughters and sons of God. This is the enduring power of divine love. In the name of Jesus Christ, your sins are completely and irrevocably forgiven. Be at peace. Amen." It brings to mind a little wet poem by Philip Larkin:

---

9. This is the phrase John Calvin used to describe how Christ absolves us by taking upon himself our sins, writing, "This is the wonderful exchange which, out of his measureless benevolence, he has made with us; that, becoming Son of man with us, he has made us sons of God with him; that, by his descent to earth, he has prepared an ascent to heaven for us; that, by taking on our mortality, he has conferred his immortality upon us; that, accepting our weakness, he has strengthened us by his power; that, receiving our poverty unto himself, he has transferred his wealth to us; that, taking the weight of our iniquity upon himself . . . he has clothed us with his righteousness." Although written in the context of his reflections on the Lord's Supper, it is appropriate for an understanding of baptism as well. See Calvin, *Institutes* (trans. Battles), 2:1362.

Water

> If I were called in
> To construct a religion
> I should make use of water.
>
> Going to church
> Would entail a fording
> To dry, different clothes;
>
> My liturgy would employ
> Images of sousing,
> A furious devout drench,
>
> And I should raise in the east
> A glass of water
> Where any-angled light
> Would congregate endlessly.[10]

One day we may continue this series of sacramental experiments by borrowing an idea attributed to Marva Dawn. At the beginning of worship (immediately following the prelude when the room is silent) someone will walk in carrying a large pitcher of water, empty it slowly and deliberately into the baptismal font and say, "The waters of our identity." A second person will then walk in bringing a chalice and paten, set them on the communion table, and announce, "The feast of our future." A third person will enter with a Bible in hand, place and open it on the pulpit and proclaim, "The book of our story." Finally, I will walk in, and with open arms and a warm smile say, "People of God, welcome home!"

Since I hail from a tradition that does not rebaptize, we have looked for such ways to help people remember their baptisms, and to renew the baptismal covenant through the reaffirmation of vows. A version of Wesley's Covenant Renewal Service is typically

---

10. Larkin, *The Whitsun Weddings*, 20.

celebrated annually on *Baptism of the Lord Sunday*, soon after the New Year. Our adaptation of it over the years has variously included such things as inviting people forward to select a smooth stone from the brimming font, or tracing the sign of the cross on their foreheads with water from the font. No fewer than three times in every worship service there is an allusion to baptism that has been integrated into the liturgy. The first occurrence is in the singing of the doxology ("Praise Father, Son, and Holy Ghost"). The second one signals the end of a sermon ("In the name of the Father and of the Son and of the Holy Spirit. Amen."). And the last one happens at the benediction: following the Aaronic blessing (Num 6:24–26), while making the sign of the cross over the congregation, I say, "In the name of God the Father, God the Son, and God the Holy Spirit." Each instance, with its echoes of the baptismal formula, is intended to reinforce sacramental identity and imagination.

As a final example, when we celebrate funerals, the closing words of the service are spoken from the font. While water is being splashed and sprinkled on people in the first few rows, the celebrant says, "In sure and certain hope of the resurrection to eternal life, I declare to you that *Name* has now completed *his/her* baptism. Blessed are the dead who die in the Lord, says the Spirit. They rest from their labors, and their works follow them" (Rev 14:13). This liturgical act bookends a person's life, from beginning to end, in sacramental language, and encourages the survivors to live the remainder of their days in such a way as to end their lives well, until baptism-complete.

After being exposed to such language and images for nearly two decades I was curious to find out if members of my own congregation had found it to be a helpful rubric for discipleship formation. Following is a representative sampling of those findings.

A staff member described the way baptism helps to even out the hierarchies of power, education, income, and age. Noting that we are a highly educated congregation located near a university town, he commented on our decision to remove all titles from people's names, not only omitting "Dr." and "Rev.," but even "Mr. and Mrs.," so as not to set people apart by occupation, education, or marital status. The idea is that the titles and roles that create prestige in our culture are meaningless in the kingdom, where the first shall be last. The personal names uttered over the waters at baptism are sufficient, identifying each of us as members in the one family of God where there are no favorite children. This *leveling effect* of baptism has helped us to more effectively minister as a priesthood of all believers.

Another member spoke of the way baptism has created something of a hermeneutic for her life, affecting the way she reads Scripture, and informing the way she pursues her vocation.

Yet another person expressed appreciation for the way baptism connects us to a covenant way of life, especially in marriage.

Lastly, one of the pleasant surprises that came out of this meeting was hearing a new staff member (just three months on the payroll) articulate baptism as something that is "practiced," as a way of life. It is, she said, "a current, daily part of our lives, rather than a one-time event at the beginning of our journey." That she picked this up in the context of worship in a relatively short period of time was gratifying. Not everyone, however, has been so quick to recognize its value.

I became aware of a man in our fellowship who, while being deeply pious and committed to Christ, has never felt the need either to be baptized or to join our church, although he has been a faithful participant since its inception. I was interested in understanding why that was the case, but also what it is like for him to be in an environment where baptism is a recurrent theme. "Jackson" was raised in a Nazarene Church, and understands baptism as an individual's expression before the community reflecting an inner, personal commitment to follow Christ. He views it, therefore, more as a public testimony, witnessing to the decision to live a life of discipleship. In his case, he had a profound conversion experience during his first year of college, but instead of being baptized, he gave his testimony to his congregation, and sees that as his rite of initiation into the body of Christ. In his own words, "the act of getting wet is merely symbolic of an inner reality which can be effected in other ways, as through a public profession of faith."

Still, he described our emphasis on baptism in words such as "refreshing" and "intriguing," and expressed his appreciation for the continual reminder on those occasions when vows are renewed. When asked how it is for him to hear the baptism-specific language common in our setting he said that at first it sounded judgmental, and he wondered if people might think that he wasn't saved. Over time, however, he learned simply to do some internal "translating," so that when he hears *baptism* he thinks *conversion* or *discipleship*. And when asked why, even now, he chooses not to be baptized, he said that he still could, but doesn't see the need for it, reiterating his sense that it is symbolic of a commitment to Christ, not a necessary act for discipleship. He went on to remind me that "there was that man who was crucified next to Jesus who was saved and welcomed into paradise without benefit of being baptized." Point taken from the Penitent Thief.

It is gratifying to see additional evidence of how the people who comprise the community known as Colbert Presbyterian Church are integrating baptismal imagination in their own lives. For example, a recent email that came through our prayer chain said, "Thank you for your prayers for my Aunt Nancy during her long illness. She completed her baptism last night, surrounded by her family and a Great Cloud of Witnesses." Even so brief a note as that provides the reminder that we are all going to die someday, and every day until that fateful day arrives presents additional opportunities to live out a baptismal identity. It is, additionally satisfying to hear the stories of people who have found baptism to be meaningful, helpful, even salvific.

A young man recently shared with me his experience of traveling in a foreign country, driven, he said, by his desire to "run away from home." As it happened, what he was running from kept catching up to him, even thousands of miles away, because it was within him. After several weeks of fleeing he was exhausted, defeated, despondent. He had nowhere to go, no place to hide. He was at the end of his rope. In fact, he found himself staring at the end of a rope one day, contemplating putting an end to his life. He spent some time reflecting on how it had come to this, having arrived at a point where he no longer wanted to live. In the wake of his considerable regrets, death was looking like a merciful friend of deliverance from his pain. "And then," he said to me, "just when it could not have gotten any darker, what I heard was as clear as my voice speaking to you right now: *You are baptized!*" That was all he heard, but it was all he needed. He cut the rope down, and boarded the next plane for home, whereupon he began the long, hard work of reconciling his relationships. The rope he retained as a reminder that what nearly ended his life became a lifeline, rescuing him from the noose, and restoring him to the covenant of his baptismal identity and purpose.

I will never forget the story of a friend who failed hospice. At the age of fifty-seven, after her doctors gave her something short of six months to live, Sandy quit her job, and moved in with her daughter and grandchildren to finish out her days. To the bewilderment of her doctors she didn't die. She was healed. Without chemotherapy, radiation, surgery, or even so much as an aspirin, she was, according to her testimony, "cured by the Great Physician." Since then, a friend of hers has sent a card on each of her birthdays to celebrate her new life. The cards commemorate not her actual age, but the years since being given a second chance at life. The last card she received celebrated her "eleventh" birthday.

Like a lot of people who have had similar experiences, Sandy sees her close encounter with death as a gift that has more fully ushered her into an abundant way of life, characterized, in my observation, by an indomitably joyful spirit. You will never hear her complain about the weather, or about traffic, or any of the other things that can cause people to grumble. She doesn't have time for such petty complaints; she is too busy being grateful, living her life fully whether in traffic jams by herself or at Mariners' games with her family. Significantly, her life is primarily focused on and defined by people. It is in relationships, she has found, that she experiences the greatest meaning and the deepest joy. This is the mysterious way of baptism: only by entering into solidarity with Jesus in his death is one able to fully experience the fullness of life he came to bring.

While conducting field research for this project I had the
pleasure of meeting and interviewing a number of practitioners
who are being intentional about integrating lively baptismal identity in their respective congregations. Through conversations with
these leaders I posed questions around the *why* and *how* of discipleship formation using the sacrament of baptism as its primary
pedagogical tool. I was eager to hear stories of how these leaders
landed on baptism as a focal point for their ministries, how they
have experienced baptism being an agent of transformation and
renewal, and how they keep baptismal identity alive and fresh in
their congregational contexts. Because of the relatively small per-
centage of pastors who are doing this, I was interested in understanding just why they consider a recovery of the catechumenate
preferable to the plethora of leadership literature that is popular
among so many colleagues.

Paul Palumbo, whom I met at the NAAC training conference
mentioned earlier, has been using the catechumenal process to
great benefit in his Lake Chelan congregation for the last sixteen
years—long enough to judge its value. During that time 80 percent
of the members have gone through the process. Additionally, he
said that becoming a sponsor to a catechumen is a great way to
keep their own baptism alive and fresh.

Paul's love of the catechumenate is apparent as he describes
the process. Through a series of classes, he unpacks one aspect of
the Sunday liturgy each week, and shows how it can be practiced
outside of worship. The *Kyrie*, which he shared at the NAAC conference, is but one way that a piece of the Sunday liturgy, practiced
week after week, can be integrated into one's life. One person told
him of an experiment she tried that grew to become a holy habit.
Whenever she has to stop for a traffic signal, its three lights prompt
her to affirm aloud that part of the communion liturgy commonly
known as the Paschal Mystery, namely,

> Christ has died.
> Christ has risen.
> Christ will come again.

It reminds her, she says, that she has a share in the death, resurrection, and return of Christ.

I had an especially delightful conversation with Linda Nepsted, pastor of the church my father founded in 1963—the year I was born. When I returned to Christ Our King Presbyterian Church for its fiftieth anniversary celebration in 2013 (the first time I had been back since my ordination in 1990) there was much about the weekend that was meaningful. At the evening gala, I was asked to reflect on my experience of having grown up in that church, and the formative environment it was for me. I mentioned the role of my Sunday School teachers, the youth group, and the adult men who mentored me. I emphasized that it all began with my baptism, and I took the opportunity to thank them for the faithful ways they helped to raise me in the fear and the admonition of the Lord. One result of those reflections, Linda later told me, is that a ten-year-old boy named Parker has decided that he now wants to be a pastor. Every Sunday after worship, as people are filing out of the sanctuary and heading for the coffee, Parker heads to the pulpit to practice his preaching, and then he splashes water in the font. He's always the last one to leave.

The moment from that weekend that haunted me, however, was when the associate pastor began the Sunday morning worship service. Standing at the font he poured a copious amount of water into the clear glass bowl and simply said, "All who are thirsty, come to the Living Water." I was very curious to learn how this came to be, for nothing like it had ever happened in the first three decades of that church's life. Linda explained that the choir director and two choir members had attended a worship conference at Montreat where the leader had started each service in this way and they came back extremely enthused and became insistent that this was something their church should adopt. Linda shared with me that she was actually resistant to the idea initially, even opposed to it. But after a couple of years, which included the conversions and baptisms of both a Jewish man and a Hindu man, she saw the effect it had on the congregation as these two men not only renounced sin and evil but paid the hefty price of leaving behind their families and traditions in order to be followers of Jesus. This, she said, was the catalyst for integrating baptismal identity throughout the congregation.

Kelly, another member I spoke with, was one of the elders who attended the Montreat Conference on worship where this baptismal seed was first planted. Particularly meaningful to her was when the leader dunked cedar branches in the font and walked down the aisles, shaking the water onto the people. It was largely due to Kelly's enthusiasm that prompted the restoration of the font as a focal point of liturgy at Christ Our King.

The liturgy has varied a bit over the ten years that this congregation has been emphasizing baptism, but they have now landed on something quite simple. It goes like this: at the beginning of each worship service the ruling elder who is assisting that day approaches the font and says, "Christ is our Prophet, Priest, and King." A large pitcher of water is then poured slowly into the clear, glass bowl, followed by this simple invitation to worship: "Come to the Living Water!" As Kelly further reflected on this she said that every time this happens it reminds her of her own testimony that "Jesus Christ is Lord" and it centers her in Christ, preparing her for another week of living her faith.

That simple liturgy leads me to wonder if there is a way to more frequently evoke images from the Prayer of Thanksgiving over the Water on occasions other than when the sacrament itself is observed. Focusing on the gift of water, the prayer mentions the Spirit's work in bringing order out of the watery chaos; of the floodwaters in Noah's time; of Israel's safe passage through the Red Sea; of Jesus' baptism in the Jordan; and the pouring out of the Holy Spirit on those who have been grafted into Christ. Stained glass images of these great events, once common in churches and cathedrals, are rarely seen in more modern sanctuaries. Perhaps it is time for a different guild of artisans to be commissioned to portray anew the baptismal signs of our story, helping to recover our sacramental sensibilities.

Throughout its life, the church has always sought ways to help people integrate baptismal imagination. One of the more enduring examples is the introduction and widespread use of the eight-sided font. Beginning as early as the fourth century, baptismal fonts were designed with eight sides, suggestive of the ways the baptized are people of the "eighth day." Ambrose, who baptized Augustine, pointed out that "not only is the font octagonal, but the baptistry [the building that houses it] as well, because on the eighth day, by rising, Christ loosens the bondage of death and receives the dead from their graves *(a tumulis suscipit examines)*."[11] There are only seven days in a week, but the suggestion of an eighth day points to the transcendent truth of the way baptism ushers people from creation to re-creation, with more life yet to come. Eighth-day disciples, as they live in the high humidity conditions of their baptism, are being prepared for life in the New Jerusalem, which will have a crystal-clear river flowing through the middle of it (Rev 22:1–2). Augustine himself considered the eighth day image to be important, writing,

> And that seventh age will be our Sabbath, a day that knows no evening but is followed by the Day of the Lord, an everlasting eighth day, hallowed by the resurrection of Christ prefiguring the eternal rest, not only of the spirit, but of the body as well. Then we shall have holiday, and we shall see and we shall love, and we shall love and we shall praise. Behold, this is how it shall be at the end without end. For what else is our end but to come to that reign?[12]

And yet, how many people today, seeing an eight-sided font, would be able to point to its semiotic significance as the consummation of God's covenantal promises? One obvious way, therefore, to recover these forgotten early church treasures is through the educational process of the catechumenate.

Another connection to consider involves the relationship between baptism and marriage. Baptism is the classroom of covenant where we are instructed in the language of enduring promises, of

11. Quoted in Kuehn, *A Place for Baptism*, 55.

12. Augustine, *City of God* 22.30, quoted in Kuehn, *A Place for Baptism*, 53–54.

faithfulness, of completion. The baptismal vows we make and regularly reaffirm speak a resounding *yes* to God's preemptive choice of us. Similarly, at weddings, vows are exchanged, affirming the choices couples make to love, honor, and cherish one another for the duration of their lives together. Nobody expects a newly married couple to have a perfect marriage beginning with the return from their honeymoon. Rather, the expectation is for two imperfect people to keep choosing one another, to daily practice the living of their vows, to do the hard work of honoring their marital covenant with fidelity and grace. Just so, the newly baptized are not expected to be candidates for canonization anytime soon. Like marriage, baptism is marked by a covenant-making day and it is then characterized by the daily choices to honor the object of one's commitment. These covenant environments represent the primary arenas of God's grace where we are invited to imperfectly practice our sacred vows. In both cases—baptism and marriage—the covenantal relationship is completed and perfected only in death.

Yet another implication to consider, one mentioned in the Introduction, is related to parenting. The church in general, and the "little church" of families in particular, needs to do everything it can to raise up children of God. For many of the reasons related to formation already discussed in chapter 1, the earlier we start the better. How we *begin* affects who we *become*. I like the way my friend and mentor Leonard Sweet indirectly argues for infant baptism as a parenting responsibility.

> As parents, giving our children the freedom to choose their faith is like telling them to choose their language. At birth, parents naturally choose their children's verbal language. At baptism, parents choose their children's faith language. When children are born into a family, they learn the family name, identity, traditions, practices, life line, and character. Shared stories and songs create collective identities.[13]

The metaphor I used recently when speaking to a couple about whether to dedicate or baptize their children went something like

13. Sweet, *The Well-Played Life*, 96.

this: from the very beginning of our lives decisions were made on our behalf by our parents, representing our best interests. Our parents decide what kind of food we're going to eat, what clothes we're going to wear, and when bedtime is. As we get older, we begin to make those decisions for ourselves, but if they were not made for us in our formative years we would not have a foundation for making good choices; indeed, we wouldn't have survived in the first place. In my family, education is highly valued. Because it is my expectation that my children will pursue higher education beyond high school, I have assumed the responsibility of setting up college funds for each of them, and I deposit money in them every month. I've been doing this since they were quite young. Although I didn't know where they would go to college, or even *if* they would, I made preparations for them, providing a financial foundation, along with the expectation that their formal education would not stop with a high school diploma.

In the same way that parents encourage educational pursuits in their children and prepare them to be contributing citizens in this world, bringing them to the waters of baptism and training them in the ways of righteousness make up the environment that forms them to be citizens of the kingdom of heaven.

I join Aidan Kavanaugh in saying,

> I shall take confidence that the restored Roman rites of Christian Initiation have begun to come alive when I read a treatise on Christian ethics that begins with baptism into Christ; when I see episcopal meetings deciding on Church discipline from a baptismal perspective; when I partake in ecumenical discussions that begin not with Luther or Cranmer or Calvin or Trent, but with baptism; when I am lectured on ministry in terms not of modern sexual roles but of baptism; when I can worship in a parish that consummates its corporate life through Lent at the paschal vigil, gathered around the font where all new life begins.[14]

14. Johnson, *The Rites of Christian Initiation*, 478.

Whatever it looks like, it involves what Wendell Berry describes as a "long choosing"—the continual choices, big and small that both renounce sin and evil and affirm faith in Christ. Andy, one of Berry's fictitious characters, reflects on the formative effects of those choices on his life.

> On the verge of his journey, he is thinking about choice and chance, about the disappearance of chance into choice, though the choice be as blind as chance. That he is who he is and no one else is the result of a long choosing, chosen and chosen again. He thinks of the long dance of men and women behind him, most of whom he never knew, some he knew, two he yet knows, who choosing one another chose him. He thinks of the choices, too, by which he chose himself as he is now. How many choices, how much chance, how much error, how much hope have made that place and people that, in turn, made him? He does not know. He knows that some who might have left chose to stay, and that some who did leave chose to return, and he is one of them. Those choices have formed in time and place the pattern of membership that chose him, yet left him free until he should choose it which he did once, and now has done again.[15]

The summation of one's life, as Berry suggests, is the accumulating result of the choices made over the span of a lifetime, some of which are made for us, and others by us, but all of which are consequential to the outcome of our lives. Put another way, "we are creatures designed for relationship, and either we are shaped by the relationships that choose us or we choose the relationships on the basis of the person we intend to become."[16] Being anchored in baptismal identity and purpose enables individuals (and whole communities of people) to move within a sacred framework from which to make holy choices, resulting in meaningful, holy lives. More like swimming than walking, this is the sacred movement of a journey toward Christ, and the integrative process of becoming more and more like him.

15. Berry, *Remembering*, 60.
16. McManus, *The Artisan Soul*, 118.

6

The Signs and Seals of Deliverance

But we, who have undertaken god, can never finish.
—RAINER MARIA RILKE

When you put your hand in the flowing stream,
you touch the last that has gone before and the first of what is to come.
—LEONARDO DA VINCI

Thus we see now what in these days God calls us to. We are now
planted by the waters in which some Christians wade to the ankles
(and be we thankful for that), some can but creep, as it were in the
way of grace, and some, it may be, can walk on with some strength;
some have yet gone deeper, till they be wholly drenched in grace,
and this should we all labor after.
—JOHN COTTON, *WAY OF LIFE OR GOD'S WAY AND COURSE*
[1641]

I SHALL NEVER FORGET the scene. With a mug of black coffee in
hand, I was on a walk through my woodsy, rural neighborhood
early one spring morning. As the sun began to bathe the landscape

with light I came over a hill and was able to look down into a horse corral where I saw my neighbor, Mary, hunched over a foal. As I came closer it became apparent that the foal had just been born: she was unsteady on her hooves and still wet. While the mother mare stood close by and kept a watchful eye, Mary straddled the foal, pressing her face up against the side of the newborn's face, vigorously rubbing its neck. I had never seen anything quite like it before, but it all looked very intimate, up close, personal, even affectionate.

A day or two later when I ran into Mary at the post office I asked her about that peculiar morning. "What was the thing you were doing the other day with that foal"? Very matter-of-factly, almost as if she was annoyed to have to explain such a thing to a city boy, Mary responded with a single word: "Imprinting." Seeing that the word wasn't registering for me, she continued: "If, in the first hours of its life, a horse is exposed to you, where it gets your smell, and hears your voice, it's much easier to train as it grows up. From now on I'm like a surrogate mother to that horse, and it will respond to my voice, and trust me to lead it. We've bonded."

Imprinting. A deep and meaningful relationship with God begins with our baptism into Christ, where we get acquainted with the voice of the Son, where we become familiar with his ways. And it develops as we practice our baptisms, entering the rhythms of a life of discipleship, most significantly as we exercise the holy affirmations and the holy denials of our new life: "No" to sin and evil; "Yes" to the kingdom of God and the Jesus way. We hear the voice; we heed the voice. We get trained up in righteousness, and we become increasingly intimate with the lover of our souls.

From the time when we are still wet behind the ears, we are influenced and formed by other people. Observations concerning infants reveal that they begin to mirror their mother's facial expressions long before they can speak their first word. As children mature it becomes apparent that they are unnervingly astute, observing and then imitating the behaviors they are exposed to, both for good and for bad.

Imitating others does not end once one reaches physical maturity. We continue to be influenced by others around us, and we have a strong tendency to adopt various versions of their values, idiosyncrasies, and lifestyles as our own. The notion, for example, that married couples begin to look and act more similarly as the years go by is a real phenomenon, because people in long-term proximity to one another tend to mimic each other's facial expressions.

Unfortunately, healthy models showing us how to live Christianly are spotty. Almost every Christian I have ever known has, at some point, disappointed me. That, however, does not mean we should stop imitating people; it just means that we need to choose carefully, searching for men and women who are living purposefully, sacrificially, courageously, as people of truth and grace, ones in whom the fruits of the Spirit are evident. Integrity, more so than perfection, is the chief criterion in the selection of models that mime messiah.

Six hundred years ago Thomas à Kempis wrote *The Imitation of Christ*, which has become one of the most beloved of devotional classics, second only to the Bible in the number of languages into which it has been translated. Even if the book itself was never read, however, the title alone would be instructive: the goal of the Christian life is to become more and more like Jesus, so that we gradually grow to actually *manifest* him.

Nobody knows how to do this innately. Our natural instinct is to go the way of Adam, rebelling against God. Reconditioning our minds and hearts for life in the kingdom of God requires a mimetic energy influenced by the saints and other more ordinary heroes of the faith, not exactly mimicking but emulating, imitating but not copying. It avoids living one's faith vicariously through another, while modeling a life of discipleship after someone who is mature in Christ and who exhibits spiritual fruit. St. Paul claimed to be one among numerous such models for the church in Philippi when he wrote, "Brothers and sisters, join in imitating me, and observe those who live according to the example you have in us"

(Phil 3:17).[1] The letter to the church in Ephesus, however, goes directly to the source, saying, "Therefore be imitators of *God*, as beloved children, and live in love, as Christ loved us" (Eph 5:1–2; italics mine).

René Girard, the founder of mimetic theory, discovered a simple yet powerful pattern detectable in all interpersonal relationships, claiming that "imitation is the fundamental mechanism of human behavior."[2] In other words, we become and we behave like the people with whom we keep company. This is why, with both warning and encouragement, St. John wrote, "Beloved, do not imitate what is evil but imitate what is good" (3 John 11). The baptized lifestyle is the art of imitating the master artist, the one who both created all things good, and the one who is restoring goodness to all things. It is this godly mission of goodness that gets reflected in children of God as they practice the art of imitating Christ. Michael Polanyi expands on the concept:

> All arts are learned by intelligently imitating the way they are practiced by other persons in whom the learner places his confidence. To know a language is an art, carried on by tacit judgments and the practice of unspecifiable skills. The child's way of learning to speak from his adult guardians is therefore akin to the young mammal's and young bird's mimetic responses to its nurturing, protecting and guiding seniors. The tacit coefficients of speech are transmitted by inarticulate communications, passing from an authoritative person to a trusting pupil, and the power of speech to convey communication depends on the effectiveness of this mimetic transmission.[3]

This "mimetic transmission" is the art of making disciples, the journey of beginning in, and becoming like Christ.

---

1. A similar exhortation appears in 2 Thessalonians 3:7 when Paul, along with Silvanus and Timothy, wrote, "[Y]ou yourselves know how you ought to imitate us."

2. "René Girard and Mimetic Theory," Imitatio.org, n.d., accessed December 19, 2015, http://www.imitatio.org/brief-intro/.

3. Polanyi, *Personal Knowledge*, 206.

Jamie Smith, commenting on Charles Taylor's observation on the role of art, points to "a fundamental shift from art as *mimesis* to art as *poeisis*—from art *imitating* nature to art *making* its world."[4] It is the sense of the Greek word *poiema* used in the New Testament: "For we are *poems*, created in Christ Jesus for good works, which God previously prepared to be our way of life" (Eph 2:10; my translation). Like good art, disciples do not merely look good; rather, their lives have agency and are generative exhibitors of the kingdom. Good art moves us. Good poetry inspires us. Those who are baptized into Christ are God's living poems, artistic agents in the redemptive work of remaking the world. The poetic nature of baptism suggests that it is less about penmanship than it is about workmanship.

Again, this notion of becoming "like Christ" is not merely mimetic; it involves the actual participation in the very nature of Christ in the fullness of his essence. As Leonard Sweet once observed to some of his students, "[I]t is not 'imitation' but 'implantation' and 'impartation' through the hypostatic union with the Holy Spirit"[5] that is the goal of discipleship. Additionally, Sweet frequently emphasizes the notion that we are not merely *mimicking* Jesus, but *manifesting* him. The act of baptism activates us for a life that is both mimetic and poetic.

The lifelong dynamic of baptism as a lifestyle is what makes it endlessly meaningful, offering both descriptive and prescriptive language to identify not only what is, but what should be. Baptism offers a corrective (repent!) when lives lose their holy telos and aim and it provides affirmation (beloved!) when relationally reconciled. This is the tension of holding a coin on the edge of the gospel's narrow way. Baptism provides the boundaries and guardrails necessary to stay on the way with and toward Jesus.

People who are splashed in the waters of baptism grow to develop their sacramental sensibilities; they become alert to the variety of smells, sounds, sights, tastes, and feelings associated with water and its semiotic significance, recognizing that "everything in

4. Smith, *How (Not) To Be Secular*, 74.

5. From an online class discussion that took place on February 9, 2015.

it is charged with value and encoded with meanings."[6] Each of our
five senses serves this sacred purpose: pointing to the Spirit who
brooded over the water; pointing to the One who commanded the
chaotic waters to come to order; pointing to the Son who came
dripping up out of the Jordan; all pointing to the Threesome giver
of life who is partial to water as an agent of both creation and re-
creation. As Tom Long proposes, "To be baptized is a sign that
everything we are—work and play, personality and character,
commitments and passions, family and ethnicity—is gathering up
and given shape and definition by our identity as one of God's own
children."[7] Growing into such a sacred identity is the baptismal
process, a holy lifestyle, requiring a lifetime of practice.

Beginning and Becoming

Paraphrasing anthropologist Mary Douglas (1921–2007), Leonard
Sweet provides the following metaphor:

> [A]ncient writings, such as the Hebrew Scriptures, were
> not written in linear sequences, but in circuitry. You start
> at the beginning, and end back at the beginning, but
> not the beginning where you began. Rather, you end at
> a new beginning, where you have grown and matured,
> discovered something new, and found something newly
> valued.[8]

That journey leads us ever more deeply into the discovery of
God—the author and perfecter of our "neverending" story.

The central thesis of this book has worked around and developed an understanding of baptism as both a beginning and a
becoming. As has been demonstrated, these are not altogether new
ideas, but ones in need of recovery by applying fresh language and
images (or signs and signifiers) to redirect imaginations that far
too often get culturally hijacked, leading people astray. This project

6. McEntyre. *Caring for Words in a Culture of Lies*, 78.

7. Long, *Accompany Them With Singing*, 143.

8. Sweet, *The Well-Played Life*, 46.

has attempted to restore the baptismal coin on its rightful edge, avoiding the tendency to emphasize its sense of either beginning or becoming and suggesting, rather, that it is a both/and proposition. It is the combination of catechesis and mystagogy, the integration of a rock-solid foundation with a flowing river of life.

Expanding on Augustine's personal and pastorally informed awareness that discipleship is less about striving for perfection than it is about opening oneself to the action of grace, Larry Seidentop wrote, "Even conversion in only the beginning of a difficult journey, a journey during which the new self is assailed by doubts and temptations that can be overcome only with the help of grace."[9] The same grace that assumes a newlywed couple will not have mastered the art of marriage upon their return from a honeymoon is the grace given to the newly baptized. In both instances, the vows spoken establish an "until death do us part" relationship and take a lifetime of practice to fulfill. Grace is needed at every step of the covenantal journey.

Signed, Sealed, Delivered

When the prophet Jeremiah bought the field at Anathoth—a demonstration of God's purchasing power to *deliver* Israel from Babylonian warfare—he "*signed* the deed, *sealed* it, got witnesses" (Jer 32:10; italics mine) for the purpose of establishing a covenantal relationship. The enduring purpose of that covenant, though taking a variety of forms over the years, was essentially unchanged in its intent, as summarized by Jeremiah:

> They shall be my people, and I will be their God. I will give them one heart and one way, that they may fear me for all time, for their own good and the good of their children after them. I will make an everlasting covenant with them, never to draw back from doing good to them; and I will put the fear of me in their hearts, so that they may not turn from me. (Jer 32:38–40)

9. Seidentop, *Inventing The Individual*, 103.

The words "signed, sealed, delivered" as pertaining to a land contract are the descriptive metaphors for a life in Christ that are enacted and effected in baptism. I consider them in turn.

Signed

Included among Britain's nineteenth-century literary circles were collectors of authors' autographs. It was a popular pastime that involved acquiring the signatures of popular writers, not unlike other hobbyists who collect baseball cards, stamps, or coins. The significance of the signature, however, lay in its semiotic connection to the author in perpetuity. As Josh Lauer once claimed, "[W]hereas writing makes language visible, signing renders the author present and, under the proper conditions of textual belief, immortal."[10] In very real ways, authors remain present to us through their words. Signing their works maintains the connection between the writer and what they wrote.

A collection of sixty-six books comprise the canon of inspired Scripture, each one an important piece of divine communique. Although most are attributable to particular historical figures—notably, Moses, David, Isaiah, and Paul—the church has understood those writers to be mere agents of the true author, as they went about their work of transcribing the Word of God.

Baptism is the sign of the divine autograph, inscribed, not on pages, but carved in hearts. The baptized are the living signatures of the author and the editor of our faith. Moreover, the collective church community comprises an autograph album, assigned with a sacred mission, revealing the signs of God's presence, marking the world with the indelible ink of water. Or, to rotate the prism slightly, God is an autograph collector, and each name, once dipped in the water, is added to the "Lamb's book of life" (Rev 21:27). God is not satisfied until the pages are full of the personal names of the baptized, embossed for eternity in the threefold name.

10. Parker, "Material Women," 275.

When God instructed Moses to bless Aaron and his sons with what is commonly known today as the "Aaronic blessing," it was followed by this often-overlooked bit of divine commentary: "So they shall *put my name* on the Israelites, and I will bless them" (Num 6:27; italics mine). This is what happens in the sacrament of baptism: God's name is placed on our given names, naming us for our beginnings, destining us for our future becomings. Additionally, "the Greek phrase 'into the name of' (*eis to onoma*) occurs mainly in commercial or legal documents and carries the idea of 'into the ownership or possession' of someone."[11] The divine name, by which we are claimed and adopted as the children of God, grafts us into the family-of-God tree.

Names are important. *Our* names are important, as are the names we associate with, both for the ways they identify us and how they influence us. The Bible is full of them, including genealogies—generational lists of names, one after another—celebrating the interpersonal and connectional nature of our lives, naming the people to whom we owe our very existence. Moreover, each name represents not only a particular life but a specific identity. Thus, Adam was "of the ground"; Moses was "drawn out" of water; Isaac "laughed"; and Jesus "saves." Addressing a person by using their proper name honors the unique gifts assigned to them. Thus, "The friends send you their greetings. Greet the friends there, each *by name*" (3 John 15; italics mine).

However, it is increasingly rare in the modern age for names to be accompanied with such identity and purpose. The power of being baptized in the *threesome* name, therefore, is an act that imparts a *gladsome* identity to persons no matter their given name. Any Tom, Dick, or Jane can live by the sign of Father, Son, and Spirit.

And yet, as the voice of God spoke from the heavens at Jesus' baptism, it is significant to notice that his name was not used, but rather his relationship to the Father: "[T]his is my beloved *Son*, with whom I am well pleased" (Matt 3:17 // Mark 1:11 // and Luke 3:22). The primary sign of the baptized is found, not in their given

---

11. Ferguson, *Baptism in the Early Church*, 135.

name, but in the experience of being given into adoption as the daughters and sons of "Abba, Father."[12]

Similarly, when the Evangelist speaks of the saving agency of Jesus' atonement he does not refer to him in functional terms like Christ or Messiah, but in terms of his relationship to the Father: "For God so love the world that he gave his only *Son* . . . " (John 3:16; italics mine). By emphasizing this relational quality, baptism protects people from the erosive effects of reification in which their worth is reduced to their capacity for production and acquisition.

In nearly every epistle attributed to him, the Apostle Paul begins his letters with a greeting that celebrates his intended audience in the glowing terms of "saints" and only then moves into more confrontational language (Galatians is the notable exception). What initially can seem like a bait and switch, where he starts with commendations and then quickly shifts into criticism, is actually one and the same and the latter naturally follows the former. By first reminding them of their fundamental identity, Paul is showing them how they ought to live. The primary motivation for living a life of morality emerges from this baptismal identity. Only when we know who we are can we make decisions that best honor our genuine self, rather than merely following somebody else's rules and expectations. Essentially Paul is saying, "You are the *holy* ones; now *live* like it!" The baptized are the living signatures, walking endorsements of the God in whose name they are claimed.

Sealed

When Jezebel was intent on helping her husband, King Ahab, acquire a neighboring vineyard that was not for sale, she wrote letters, giving orders to the elders and nobles to kill Naboth, the owner of the vineyard. After writing the letters she "sealed them with his seal" (1 Kgs 21:8), giving them the weight and authority of the king. Although Jezebel inappropriately impersonated

12. Cf. especially Rom 8:15, and Gal 4:5–6 where adopted children are encouraged to address God with the more familiar and intimate term, *Abba*, sometimes translated as "Daddy" or "Papa."

Ahab, the orders were carried out nonetheless because they were believed to be from the king as evidenced by their accompanying seal. Baptism accompanies us with the weight of the divine seal, the assurance of being *bona fide* children of God.

Years later, when Jesus admonished his followers to work "for the food that endures for eternal life, which the Son of Man will give you," he went on to make the self-referential claim that "it is on him that God the Father has set his *seal*" (John 6:27; italics mine). The sense of the word (*sphragidzō*) is that of setting an identifying mark on a person. It may be that, according to John's Gospel, which actually has no explicit reference to Jesus' baptism, the seal he was referring to was the Holy Spirit, for as the Baptist relayed the words he heard from God, "He on whom you see the Spirit descend and remain is the one who baptizes with the Holy Spirit." John concludes, "And I myself have seen and have testified that this is the Son of God" (John 1:33–34).

A similar sense of the word appears in the letter to the Ephesians. Referring to their belief in Christ, the writer claims that they "were marked with the *seal* of the promised Holy Spirit" (Eph 1:13; italics mine). Again, equating the Spirit with the seal of God's approval, the writer adds, "[D]o not grieve the Holy Spirit of God, with which you were marked with a *seal* for the day of redemption" (Eph 4:30; italics mine).

Paul makes the same correlation in his second letter to the Corinthians, writing, "But it is God who establishes us with you in Christ and has anointed us, by putting his *seal* on us and giving us his *Spirit* in our hearts as a first installment" (2 Cor 1:22; italics mine). The Holy Spirit sets its sacred seal of approval on the baptized, as evidenced by the fruits of the Spirit they bear.

The image gets further elaborated in the Revelation where John of Patmos saw in a vision an angel who, as it ascended, cried out to four other angels, "Do not damage the earth or the sea or the trees, until we have marked the servants of our God with a seal on their foreheads" (Rev 7:3). While there is little scholarly consensus as to just what that seal looks like, the baptismal "seal" represents the very thing indicated, namely, ritual marking that sets people apart. This, by the way, is why some rites of blessing call for anointing oil to be traced in the sign of the cross on a person's forehead, along with the words, "You have been sealed by the Holy Spirit in baptism, and grafted into Christ forever."

As the sign of circumcision was, under the old covenant, the recognizable seal of righteousness (cf. Rom 4:11), baptism is the new covenant sign marking the faithful with the seal of divine approval.

Delivered

In describing the grand miracle of the atonement, C. S. Lewis introduces first one, then another parable to illustrate the effect of Christ's life, death, resurrection, ascension, and present reign on humanity—images both of which reflect the personal and intimate nature of salvation and the necessity for divine intervention. It is like a power lifter, he says, who stoops under the weight of a great burden, almost to the point of disappearing, and then straightens his back to lift it up. Lewis then shifts the images from the gym of weightlifting to an exquisite metaphor of the waters of baptism.

> Or one may think of a diver, first reducing himself to nakedness, then glancing in mid-air, then gone with a splash, vanished, rushing down through green and warm water into black and cold water, down through increasing pressure into the death-like region of ooze and slime and old decay; then up again, back to colour and light, his lungs almost bursting, till suddenly he breaks the surface again, holding in his hand the dripping, precious thing that he went down to recover.[13]

God in Christ, through a magnificent visitation of love, stoops from the heavens and dives through the slime of sin to reach us, recovering the "dripping, precious thing" that we once were and making us just so once again.

13. Lewis, *Miracles*, 148.

But it's not long before many people start to feel wrung out, dry, spiritually arid. Baptism is continually calling us to return to the waters, to reconstitute our dehydrated souls through the practices of discipleship, restoring our identity as "dripping, precious" people. Those disciplines, as this book has proposed, involves the primary movements of turning.

> God delivers us from sin and death, and we, therefore, keep turning from the ways of sin and other forms of bondage.

> God delivers us for salvation and life, and we, therefore, keep choosing the way of Jesus who is leading us into places of Promise.

This "special delivery" of salvation, additionally, signifies the altogether non-transactional nature of one's new and renewing identity in Christ. And so, while Joseph was purchased for twenty pieces of silver (Gen 37:28), and Jesus was obtained for thirty pieces of silver (Matt 26:15), the baptized—though ransomed—cannot be bought. Divine deliverance is duty-free.

Conclusion

Michael's struggle is everybody's struggle, one that remains just as real and universal today as when the ancient Akkadians carved out their creation myth on a stone slab five thousand years ago. The struggle and its ultimate resolution may be summed up best by Augustine's confession: "[Y]ou have made us for yourself, and our hearts are restless until they can find peace in you."[14] Baptism, rather than altogether remedying our restless hearts, points beyond this life, with its myriad imperfections, to the fullness of the kingdom of God where human desire is ultimately met and satisfied in the eternal presence of the Trinity: chaos giving way to a new order. Until that day, the gift of restlessness is in its power to nudge us nearer to Christ. Our inability to be completely content in this life is what prepares us to be embraced by perfect and

14. Augustine, *Confessions*, 1.1 (trans. Warner, 17).

enduring rest. Such is our telos, an end goal that cannot (by design) be fulfilled this side of the *parousia*, but one that is even now signaled by a voice from that future day, a voice speaking from our heavenly home, saying, "Write this: Blessed are the dead who from now on die in the Lord." "Yes," says the Spirit, "they will rest from their labors, for their deeds follow them" (Rev 14:13). Baptism is what allows people, living between the two advents of Christ, to make sense of and to endure the crucible-like nature of the *present*, in order to inherit resurrection in the *future*.

It has been ten years now since I baptized Michael. When I asked him about it recently he reflected that, while his baptism has not delivered him from the struggles, it has made his struggles more meaningful. By locating his life in the sacramental waters of baptism, he has found that he is more apt and able to remain engaged in the worthy struggle of contending with principalities and powers, while also cooperating with the grace of God. The two fundamental words in the lexicon of baptism (*no* and *yes*) are not new to him. However, his ability to live his faith through the practice of renunciations and affirmations is, he says, what has ushered him more deeply into a life of abundance.

Michael's testimony reminds me that not only is baptism the sign of our faith but in living out of such a baptismal identity we ourselves become more and more the living signs of God's enduring presence and abiding love. There is nothing like baptism that has both the power and the sacramental authority to claim people who have become resigned to lives of futility and reassigning them for lives of abundance in the kingdom of God, making it the chief semiotic of salvation.

Baptism enlarges our vision, inviting people to enter into and to participate in a reality as broad and eternal as the kingdom of God itself. This increased capacity of our humanity is perhaps what Jesus was referring to when he said, "I came that they may have life, and have it abundantly" (John 10:10). The way of abundant life is the baptized way of life: signed, sealed, delivered.

Once you start looking for it, it's quite amazing to see how pervasive baptismal images are.

An ancient proverb tells the story of a girl whose morning chore it was to walk to the river and fetch water for her household. Suspended from a pole across her shoulders were two water pots that supplied her family's daily needs. One of the pots was perfect, but the other one was cracked, and by the time they made the return trip home each day, the second pot was only half full.

After some time, the little cracked pot, ashamed that she wasn't able to function at full capacity, expressed her embarrassment and sense of failure to the girl. "Why do you keep using me when all I do is leak?" she asked. "Why don't you replace me with a new pot?" Smiling, the girl gently responded, "Have you seen the beautiful flowers that grow along the path between the house and the river? And have you noticed that they only grow on your side of the path as we walk home together? That's because every spring I plant seeds on only your side, knowing that you will water them as we walk home together. I've been picking those flowers for years and filling our home with fragrance and beauty. I couldn't do it without you. What you thought was a flaw is actually a gift to us all."

In ways that both confound and astound me, God consistently chooses to accomplish divine purposes through the agency of human imperfection. Through the weaknesses and shortcomings of the clay pots—which are our lives—uncommonly beautiful things emerge. Consider one of the apostle's favorite metaphors: "We have this treasure in clay jars, so that it may be made clear that this extraordinary power belongs to God and does not come from us" (2 Cor 4:7). It's the mystery that the treasure of salvation is being held in the container of the earthen vessels of the sons and daughters of Adam and Eve—children of the *ground*. While God could have selected much more dependable, durable vessels—made of stainless steel or titanium, for example—God chooses instead to stick close to the ground. He chooses us: pottered people, full of faults and blemishes. God accomplishes extraordinary things through quite ordinary, faulty people. As the linguist Edward Sapir famously remarked, "[A]ll grammars leak," so too all baptized people leak.[15]

15. Sapir, *Language*, 39.

Jesus himself incarnated this way of life. From the occasion when he wept at the tomb of Lazarus, to the gash in his side on the cross, he leaked his life into this world. Jesus poured himself out as a liquid love offering, as do those who have been baptized in his name.

In a world full of despots who are full of only themselves, I place my trust these days in the crackpots of this world who overflow with the fruits of the Spirit. The treasure of salvation is a gift to receive and hold, but not one to contain and hoard. It's only a complete gift when it flows. People of the baptized way leak life, spilling grace and beauty into an otherwise bland and barren world, such that what at first appears to be an embarrassing design flaw is actually in accordance with divine intent.

From one crackpot to another, I pray that your remaining days are especially lovely, leaky ones, until you are found—with all the saints—baptism-complete!

Epilogue

THIS IS DEEPLY PERSONAL for me. I was baptized by my pastor-father on Easter Sunday, 1963 when I was two months old. Since then, in fits and starts, I have been guided into the life of discipleship through a number of godly people, as I have gradually "learned Christ" (Eph 4:20). While the actual memory of my baptismal day is held mostly by the people who held my infant body on that sacred occasion, my baptismal identity has held me in the container of God's love, and has expanded in significance as I have grown up in Christ, thereby increasing my capacity to both receive and convey the grace of God. I have found it to be the single most significant sacred sign, capable of ushering me into a crucified and resurrected way of life. The same eight-sided oak font from which I was claimed as a child of God over fifty years ago sits prominently in my study today, along with my baptismal certificate, as not only daily reminders of who I am and to whom I belong, but as tangible signs that point me toward the good and abundant way of life.

Significant for me is what is *not* on display: no academic diplomas, no certificates of completion, no plaques of recognition; just the evidence that I am baptized. As an identity, it is more than sufficient, for it gives me both something to live for and something to die for. No mere metaphor (which is limited to being expressive), the sacrament of baptism has the power to be enactive and participative.

I love the story of Louis IX, King of France who reigned from 1226 to 1270. When asked why he signed his name "Louis of Poissey" rather than "King Louis IX," he responded,

> I think more of the place where I was baptized [*La Collégiale Notre-Dame*] than of Rheims Cathedral where I was crowned. It is a greater thing to be a child of God than to be the ruler of a Kingdom. This last I shall lose at death, but the other will be my passport to an everlasting glory.

The quotation is cut upon the stone of the baptistery at the eponymous church in France: St. Louis in Cleveland Heights. Significantly, Louis IX is the only king who has ever been canonized.

When I began the work of organizing a new church in the summer of 1997 I had very little idea of what I was doing. While my vocational identity was already well established the task of a church "plant" was daunting, even intimidating. Failure was a continual fear of mine. I consider it no small grace during this time that I became aware of a lingering temptation within me to treat people as means to the end of a successful new church development. Attention to baptismal theology provided the blessed check and correction to this tendency toward reification by causing me to view people through a sacred lens. Happily, in all the subsequent years of wading in the water, I have been unable to fully fathom the depths of this sacred well of blessing.

The foregoing work is the fruit of that fertile congregational womb.

Eric of Baltimore
Baptism of the Lord, 2018

But friends, that's exactly who we are: children of God.
And that's only the beginning. Who knows how we'll end up!
—1 John 3:2 (MSG)

Bibliography

Badaracco, Joseph, L. *The Good Struggle: Responsible Leadership in an Unforgiving World.* Boston: Harvard Business Review, 2013.

Berkhof, Henrikus. *Christian Faith: An Introduction to the Study of the Faith.* Translated by Sierd Woudstra. Grand Rapids: Eerdmans, 1979.

Berry, Wendell. *Remembering.* San Francisco: North Point, 1988.

———. *What Are People For? Essays By Wendell Berry.* New York: North Point, 1990.

Best, Harold, M. *Unceasing Worship: Biblical Perspectives On Worship and the Arts.* Downers Grove, IL: InterVarsity, 2003.

Blake, Aaron. "Palin: 'Waterboarding is how we baptize terrorists.'" *Washington Post,* April 28, 2014. http://www.washingtonpost.com/news/post-politics/wp/2014/04/28/palin-waterboarding-is-how-we-baptize-terrorists/.

Bonhoeffer, Dietrich. *The Cost of Discipleship.* Translated by R. H. Fuller. New York: Touchstone, 1995.

Brooks, David. *The Road to Character.* New York: Random House, 2015.

Bruce, F. F. *The Epistle to The Hebrews.* New International Commentary on the New Testament. Grand Rapids: Eerdmans, 1964.

Buechner, Frederick. *Beyond Words: Daily Readings in the ABC's of Faith.* New York: HarperCollins, 2004.

———. *Wishful Thinking: A Theological ABC.* New York: Harper & Row, 1973.

Bushkofsky, Dennis, Suzanne Burke, and Richard Rouse, eds. *Go Make Disciples: An Invitation to Baptismal Living.* Minneapolis: Augsburg Fortress, 2012.

Byrne, David. *How Music Works.* San Francisco: McSweeney's, 2012.

Calvin, John. *Institutes of the Christian Religion.* Vol. 2. Edited by John T. McNeill. Translated by Ford Lewis Battles. LCC 21. Philadelphia: Westminster, 1960.

Carpenter, Delores, ed. *African American Heritage Hymnal.* Chicago: GIA, 2001.

Coakley, Sarah. *God, Sexuality, and the Self: An Essay "On the Trinity."* Cambridge: Cambridge University Press, 2013.

Ferguson, Everett. *Baptism in the Early Church: History, Theology, and Liturgy in the First Five Centuries.* Grand Rapids: Eerdmans, 2009.

Frankl, Viktor E. *Man's Search for Meaning: An Introduction to Logotherapy.* New York: Simon and Schuster, 1959.

Bibliography

Geary, James. *I Is an Other: The Secret Life of Metaphor and How It Shapes the Way We See the World*. New York: Harper Perennial, 2012.

Griffith, Paul J. "The Nature of Desire." *First Things*. December 2009. http://www.firstthings.com/article/2009/12/the-nature-of-desire.

Griswald, Frank T. "Toward a Baptismal Spirituality." In *Drenched in Grace: Essays in Baptismal Ecclesiology Inspired by the Work and Ministry of Louis Weil*, edited by Lizette Larson-Miller and Walter Knowles, 217–24. Eugene, OR: Pickwick, 2013.

Johnson, Maxwell. *The Rites of Christian Initiation: Their Evolution and Interpretation*. Collegeville, MN: Liturgical, 1989.

Kaplan, Jeffrey. "The Gospel of Consumption and the Better Future We Left Behind." *Orion* (2008) 38–47.

Keating, Daniel A. *The Appropriation of the Divine Life in Cyril of Alexandria*. Oxford: Oxford University Press, 2004.

Kuehn, Regina. *A Place for Baptism*. Chicago: Liturgy Training, 1992.

Larkin, Philip. *The Whitsun Weddings*. London: Faber & Faber, 1964.

Lewis, C. S. *Miracles*. New York: Touchstone, 1996.

Long, Thomas, G. *Accompany Them with Singing: The Christian Funeral*. Louisville: Westminster John Knox, 2009.

Luther, Martin. *Luther's Works*. Vol. 32, *Career of the Reformer II*. Edited by George W. Forrell. Translated by Charles M. Jacobs. Philadelphia: Fortress, 1958.

McEntyre, Marilyn, Chandler. *Caring for Words in a Culture of Lies*. Grand Rapids: Eerdmans, 2009.

McManus, Erwin Raphael. *The Artisan Soul: Crafting Your Life into a Work of Art*. New York: HarperOne, 2014.

Neuman, Scott. "Oliver Sacks, Renowned Neurologist and Author, Dies at 82." *National Public Radio, The Two Way*. August 30, 2015. http://www.npr.org/sections/thetwo-way/2015/08/30/436013382/oliver-sacks-renowned-neurologist-and-author-dies-at-82.

Parker, Pamela Corpron. "Woman of Letters: Elizabeth Gaskell's Autograph Collection and Victorian Celebrity." In *Material Women, 1750–1950: Consuming Desires and Collecting Practices*, edited by Maureen Daly Goggin and Beth Fowkes Tobin, 265–78. Burlington, VT: Ashgate, 2009.

Pearse, Roger. "The Tertullian Project." http://www.tertullian.org/fathers2/ANF-03/anf03-47.htm#P11294_3203205.

Peterson, Eugene, H. *Conversations: The Message Bible with its Translator*. Colorado Springs: NavPress, 2007.

Polanyi, Michael. *Personal Knowledge: Towards a Post-Critical Philosophy*. Chicago: University of Chicago Press, 1974.

Potter, Brett David. "Lady Gaga: Monstrous Love and Cultural Baptism." May 15, 2011. http://theotherjournal.com/mediation/2011/05/15/lady-gaga-monstrous-love-and-cultural-baptism/.

Pritchard, James B., ed. *The Ancient Near East, Volume I: An Anthology of Texts and Pictures*. Princeton, NJ: Princeton University Press, 1958.

Bibliography

Ricouer, Paul. *The Symbolism of Evil*. New York: Harper & Row, 1967.

Rushkoff, Douglas. *Present Shock: When Everything Happens Now*. New York: Penguin, 2013.

Sapir, Edward. *Language: An Introduction to the Study of Speech*. New York: Harcourt, Brace, 1921.

Siedentop, Larry. *Inventing The Individual: The Origins of Western Liberalism*. Cambridge, MA: Belknap, 2014.

Smith, Christopher C., and John Pattison. *Slow Church: Cultivating Community in the Patient Way of Jesus*. Downers Grove, IL: InterVarsity, 2014.

Smith, James K. A. *Desiring the Kingdom: Worship, Worldview, and Cultural Formation*. Cultural Liturgies 1. Grand Rapids: Baker Academic, 2009.

———. *How (Not) to Be Secular: Reading Charles Taylor*. Grand Rapids: Eerdmans, 2014.

Soechtig, Stephanie, dir. *Fed Up*. Weinstein, 2014.

Staniforth, Maxwell, trans. *The Apostolic Fathers: Early Christian Writings*. London: Penguin, 1968.

Sweet, Leonard. *From Tablet to Table: Where Community Is Formed and Identity Is Found*. Colorado Springs, CO: NavPress, 2015.

———. *The Well-Played Life: Why Pleasing God Doesn't Have to be Such Hard Work*. Carol Stream, IL: Tyndale Momentum, 2014.

Tertullian. *On Baptism*. Translated by Rev. S. Theswall. In *Ante-Nicene Fathers: The Writings of the Fathers Down to A.D. 325*, edited by Alexander Roberts and James Donaldson, 3:669–79. 1885. Repr., Whitefish, MT: Kessinger Legacy, 2010.

Tournier, Paul. *The Meaning of Persons*. New York: Harper & Bros., 1957.

Warner, Rex, trans. *The Confessions of St. Augustine*. New York: Penguin, 1963.

Weber, Max. *The Protestant Ethic and the Spirit of Capitalism*. Translated by Stephen Kalberg. New York: Oxford University Press, 2011.